Praises for
LIFE INTERRUPTED

"So inspiring and thought provoking! It encouraged me to write a mission statement for my life that will always remind me of my purpose in this universe."

— Dominique Stocks

"This book has many wonderful insights on life, ranging from emotions to matters of the heart. It feels absolutely real, as if I'm reading someone's actual journal. The dialogue is so genuine and spot-on. I have had some of the same thoughts as the author, except she was able to put them into words. A very engaging read!"

— Quinetta White

"*Life Interrupted* is a great inspiration to everyone the author interacts with. I thoroughly enjoyed the read and am very proud of her endeavors."

— George White

"I enjoy reading what I can relate to and *Life Interrupted* is just that. This novel hits closer to home than I expected. If you're looking for a page turner that touches on love, health, spirituality, and more, open up to the first page and enjoy the journey. It reconfirms that no matter your circumstance, to overcome starts with a positive mind."

- K. Lewis

"*Life Interrupted* is a must read that challenged me to reflect on my own life. It reminded me that everything is not perfect and the hurdles we jump are for a just cause."

- Author, Dawn Angela Mickens

"*Life Interrupted* touched me so much, especially the part regarding the realization that your life isn't your own anymore after having a child. Every decision you make will impact them. There are no instructions, however, this book confirmed my belief that with God and family/friend support, anything is possible. It takes a village and an unselfish heart to be a mother."

- Treasure Williams

"As an entrepreneur, *Life Interrupted* reminded me that God allows you to GROW and GO. When working for someone doesn't fit the mindset that GOD has given you, GOD will interrupt your LIFE. You then must step out on FAITH and give 100%, even when business is slow, you feel like you made the wrong decision, or it's not the right time. *Life Interrupted* teaches you to remember the uncomfortable setting of that mundane place you called a JOB and remember what GOD has called you to do, so you may continue to walk in PURPOSE. It's all right to excel and GROW at that job, but apply what you have learned and GO build the vision GOD has given to you. It's all right to be uncomfortable, and it's all right for life to interrupt what you thought was right for you in order to see what you are made of and what you can achieve."

- Valerie Bowden

"*Life Interrupted* so eloquently and powerfully speaks of the things that many of us have had to face when life brought overwhelming challenges. The author connects and speaks to the heart of the issues and pain that are part of having life interrupted, as well as to the triumphs that are ours for the choosing. I highly recommend this book to those who need encouragement and healing from tough circumstances! *It's hard to grow your faith inside of your comfort zone.*" #go

-Nicole Plummer

Life
INTERRUPTED

KERI STEWARD

WWW.13THANDJOAN.COM

Life Interrupted. © 2018 by Keri Steward. All rights reserved.

No part of this publication may be reproduced, distributed, or transmitted in any form or by any means, including photocopying, recording, or other electronic or mechanical methods, without the prior written permission of the publisher, except in the case of brief quotations embodied in critical reviews and certain other noncommercial uses permitted by copyright law. For permission requests, write to the publisher, addressed "Attention: Permissions Coordinator," 500 N. Michigan Avenue, Suite #600, Chicago, IL 60611.

13th & Joan books may be purchased for educational, business or sales promotional use. For information, please email the Sales Department at sales@13thandjoan.com.

Front Cover and Back Design - Sante White
Poem Excerpt - Soul
Cover Photo - M.A. Shell Davidson (photographer)
Print Interior & Typesetting - Ampersand Book Interiors

Printed in the U.S.A.

First Printing, June 2018

Library of Congress Cataloging-in-Publication Data has been applied for.

ISBN 000-0000000

Preface

WE MUST UNLEARN everything we learned. We must let go of the life we planned, in order to accept the one waiting for us. #LifeInterrupted

Life Interrupted is a book about change. When you get serious about things changing — changing things gets serious to you. When things don't go as you planned, your regularly scheduled program is disrupted. There's a shift that takes place, something you feel deep in your mind, heart, and soul, and it's something that's very hard to shake and control. It won't feel like just another day. It will be an unusual awakening taking place on the inside of you that will literally transform the world on the outside of you.

Dedication

THIS BOOK IS dedicated to my brother Jason White, who inspired me to finish what I started because tomorrow isn't promised. He, who I protected and watched over while he was here, is now watching over me. Thank you for your life's service. "Well done, thou good and faithful servant." (Matthew 25:21 KJV) I shall run on, but I thank you for the motivation, love, and laughter. I'm grateful for the thirty-four years you were given to us on earth.

TO MY MOTHER, Quinetta White, who in all her infinite wisdom provided me with the strength, courage, and wisdom to keep me going. She inspired me to pick up where she left off and worked tirelessly to make sure that we did more than survive — she made sure we thrived. Her unconditional love fills me up until it overflows into every life I touch. She taught me to not work for a living, but to live a life full of great work and to serve others selflessly and to really live while alive. My shero, who lived a life full of service to others, while fervently praying and never giving up on her children. Even these words do not do justice to describe the bond we have as mother and daughter.

To my father, who was the first man I ever loved and the first man who broke my heart. He taught me valuable lessons of forgiveness, resiliency, laughter, and second chances. I am just as proud of you as you are of me. No one in this world could have survived the things you did and because of that I never lose. I either win or learn the lesson. Failure has never been an option, only to fail forward. Thank you for being my daughter's hero, the best father and grandfather a girl could have.

To my daughters. I often believe I am your savior, but in reality, you both saved me. You inspire me to be the highest me.

You see the best in me when I feel my worst. You love me unconditionally and when the world seems dark, you two are my candlelight. Because of you, I make wiser choices today that will affect your tomorrow. I admire the childlike faith you have that God desires to forget the past, master forgiveness, freely love, seek peace, and understanding, and most importantly to never stop dreaming! To give me the crown of mother and to hear your voices say, "Mommy" is priceless. Thank you, my goddesses.

To my uncle, Daddy G, a love child, and professor of life, thank you for your support and encouragement over the years, but most of all for the love and truths you shared. You taught me to be a lifelong learner of truth, spiritual revelations, and to unlearn most of what was learned through traditions, superstition, institutions, and society. You taught me to be a free thinker and each day I strive for knowledge, truth, new experiences, and diversity. I go deeper because you challenge me to do so. We are forever connected as seed to the sower. You've helped me reap so much already and I love you.

To every woman that thought she wasn't good enough, pretty enough, or wise enough for love. You are enough. Created with every intricate detail by love and for love. May you reconnect through vertical love from the one who created you, so your lateral relationships will be full of the divine love we all desperately want and need. God bless you.

Epigraph

"Life does not come with a manual, it comes with interruptions — interruptions to shake you from the very foundations you were taught and the comfort zones you loved, in order to propel you into an area unfamiliar. Your faith, fortitude, character, and integrity are tested as you navigate through the interruptions. If you resist there will be a struggle. If you surrender, changing things grow, and growing things change, but you will grow through the pain. Don't just go through it, grow through it."

Introduction
MY AMBITION AS A WRITER

I PUT PEN TO paper to get out what felt trapped inside of me for so long. To release the thoughts and deepest emotions I tried to bury for years was therapeutic for me. Every time the pen would touch the paper, a sentence would form, and I would feel free, somehow vindicated of my own poisonous thoughts of what I thought of myself. I played small in order for others to feel big. I gave up on my dreams in order to help others build theirs, because I thought they were worth it. I didn't see the value in myself enough to pursue my own. I thought it was too late for me. I had made too many mistakes and listened to what others thought of me, and thus I began to think I was exactly who and what I was supposed to be. As I started writing, I realized that was not where I should be. Not necessarily in a physical location, but as my spirit was crying out for help through pen and paper, I started to rescue myself and the person trapped inside to break free of that mentality. I had to get out of my own way. I had to do more than just pray, and I realized my ambition as a writer would release someone else from their own prison. Courage and transparency was the fuel to my fire and knowing that this was not about me, but about someone else's freedom, helped me surrender to pen and paper with no fear. Being fearless didn't mean I wasn't scared, it meant that although I was afraid, I was going to do it anyway.

My legacy will be one of saving souls through stories that deserve to be told. What we go through in life is not a coincidence; it is orchestrated by our thoughts and actions that leads us to places that we may or may not want to be in. There's a divine intervention that our own wills can't fight against because that power is strong enough to change the course of our lives, even when we weren't planning on it. Let it take control. The more you resist it, the more you suffer.

Prologue
SANTE WHITE

One day, while flipping through an online model repository, looking for a MUSE to make my lackluster photography skills look like visual brilliance, I came across a portfolio that ignited and changed me in ways words can't clearly describe. At surface glance, the portfolio was a mash up of model LOOKS: swimsuit, fitness, glamour, fashion, and urban chic. However, I saw something so much more. I didn't see a MODEL; I saw a STATUESQUE WARRIOR. Every pose and stance came right out of the screen. It was like watching the embodiment of defiance and a fierce heart. In a word, she was ALIVE. Imagine viewing screen after screen of practiced PLASTIC mannequin styles and coming across an AMAZING, GLOWING, HOT SOUL, encased in a warm brown human form. Now, here's the most incredible part of the story. Upon speaking to her for the first time, I quickly realized she had very little recognition of any of HER own POWER. She was humble, unassuming, nonjudgmental, unafraid, and sharp as any handcrafted sword you've ever seen.

When she filled me in on the near completion of her first book, my first thoughts were, "What took you so long?" When she told me it was about her STORY, I honestly felt two emotions at once. The first was disappointment, as I went through my memory bank and remembered the times I felt I had let my little sister down by watching her make moves I believed were not beneficial to her life, but seemed to make her happy. Second, I stepped outside of my narcissism (after realizing that this wasn't about me) and realized that I was completely filled to the brim with PRIDE over Keri's accomplishment. Above her telling her story, I can't wait for the world to see what I saw a decade ago (and I was late to the party even then, so you all have a ton of catching up to do). Keri is an ancient alien of humanity, and y'all need to watch out for the second she gets her full memory of self and conquers all.

Table of CONTENTS

1: Bad Habits ....
2: Life Interrupted: Does not Mean Life Ended.....
3: Life Interrupted: New Beginnings ....
4: Life Interrupted: Our Experiences Shape Us......
5: Life Interrupted: Health is Wealth ....
6: Life Interrupted: You Stop Dreaming, you Stop Living..
7: Life Interrupted: Planting, Plowing, and Growing..
8: Love is the Greatest..
9: The Importance of Forgiveness ....
10: Rewrite the Script..
11: Religion vs. Relationship ....
12: Life Interrupted from Past to Future....................
13: Life Interrupted: First Time Parents...................

14: Life Interrupted: The Single Parent Syndrome.
15: Once was Lost, but now Free ....
16: Life Interrupted: A Relationship with Money..
17: Life Interrupted: Connecting with Souls ....
18: Life Interrupted: Career vs. Purpose...................
19: Beauty for Ashes ....
20: Some Tables Don't Turn ....
21: Life Interrupted: When you let go, they don't..
22: Life Interrupted: Something's Got a
       Hold on Me ....
23: Life Interrupted: Death ....
24: Life Interrupted: I Remember ....

1

Bad Habits

Every day I was raising children, working in Corporate America, pursuing a modeling career, and taking care of a grown man. That's what wives are supposed to do, right? "For better or for worse," were a part of the vows we said to each other. The day we said, "I do," my worst far outweighed my better, and I was beginning to feel stuck in my own marriage.

"We are what we attract," is a familiar saying most of us have heard, but what most of us don't understand is the power and root cause of that statement. We often can't see what we're in until we're out of it. As a woman, who considered herself strong, I often saw myself as healthy, confident, kind-hearted, open-minded, and willing to help others in any way I could. I had a heart and soul so pure it longed for truth. Often, I pictured myself as a superhero reaching for her cape, while getting my children ready for school. I would listen to inspirational songs, read encouraging words, while creatively throwing together a unique wardrobe for the day, and say a quick prayer before heading out the door. As I would leave our home and ask God to protect it, I would get in my car, head to work, and think about the man I left in our safe haven. "God, please let him find some work today, some stability. Something to keep him productive. I feel like I am carrying the heaviest load daily."

Dinner would be ready by the time the kids got home from school, and I got home from work. Although it was one less thing for me to do, it wasn't enough for me to settle. It made him feel like he was really doing something, and he would remind me that I should be grateful, even without his paycheck, because most women don't get that. I believe his reasoning to be true because unfortunately, there are women in this world who, for the sake of having a warm body next to them, take on all the household and financial responsibilities. I suppressed what my soul was crying out for and agreed with his thinking for the sake of not arguing, but deep down inside I knew this wasn't it for me, and yet, somehow, it became my routine.

"Why is this happening to me?" I thought. "Isn't there a law of reaping and sowing? If I'm growing, sowing love, and searching for challenging work, shouldn't I reap the benefits of that? Where's the return on my ten-year investment?" I was with an emotionally unstable human being that I truly thought I could save. In relationships, we tend to think we can change someone, or that they will eventually change because we're designed to grow. My relationship became more and more toxic, and the greatest lesson it taught me was that people are who they are, and we have two options:

1. EITHER accept them for who they are and not complain about it, or
2. ACCEPT who they are, but change the outcome of your situation by changing yourself, or changing the environment.

I realized a marriage shouldn't be, "I'm going to marry this person despite what I see," or "Because they love me, they'll change for me." How comical! How egotistical is that? Did I really think I was all that? Just think about how hard it is to change yourself? We're naturally creatures of habit, and I had the audacity to think, "I'm so dope that he'll change for me." A marriage should be, "This person has flaws. Once I marry them, is this something I can live with?" That is the question each of us should ask ourselves before jumping into a lifelong commitment. It is unfair to our significant others to try and change them, to force them to be what we envision them to be, instead of who they truly are. Once I accepted this truth, I knew it was time for me to remove myself from the equation. I knew that if I really loved this person, regardless of being legally married or not, I owed it to him and myself to set us free and allow one another to just be. Just because two people love each other doesn't mean they belong together. We can love others from a distance. I was in a relationship and feeling extremely uncomfortable. I was a prisoner in my own home, sleeping with the enemy, and yet, this life started becoming so familiar that I stayed right there.

"For some reason we fear being the powerful, creative forces we were destined to be. Instead, we hide behind the shadows of what others think in order to not shine so brightly. We believe making others comfortable is better than making them feel uncomfortable. That is the biggest lie you could ever tell yourself and a waste of your precious time while discovering who you really are. Life is too short to play small in a big world that was created by an enormous God."

- Keri Steward.

It's unfortunate the human mind does not always align with the human spirit. We begin listening to the negative thoughts and perceptions others taught us and start to believe them. What's worse, is that once this negative thinking gets into our psyche, it becomes second nature to eventually manifest the negative behavior. We begin to tell ourselves, "We are not good enough for that, so why seek it? We can't be valued, so let's stay with someone who doesn't see our value. We're not worthy of the high calling in us, so let's stop chasing our dreams. As a matter of fact, let's stop dreaming all together." We compromise on things we shouldn't. We allow life to happen to us instead of for us. We fear being challenged, stretched, and to grow as the beautiful souls we were created to be, and as such, we start to wither. We become numb to our circumstances and ignore every cry on the inside of us to do better. If a nice, stable man approached me, it would have felt foreign to me. If he was fully available, I would have felt like I can't do anything to help this person because he's not broken; he's normal. What would be there to fix? I'd run.

As I look back over my life, the educated, stable, well-to-do men didn't cut it for me. I wanted the rebellious soul and the one that had issues. He was a project for me. He was something to conquer and overcome. I then realized, after years of verbal and sometimes physical abuse, that I had started to believe the lie, "You're not good enough." By then, I was broken and stayed in the dysfunction. The truth is, the man is the stem and the woman is the flower, and she should always see her roots in him. I didn't pay attention to the strong roots that the women in my generation planted before me. Instead, I paid attention to the rotten seeds being planted inside of me.

An open letter to my flower girls wanting to bloom:

YOU ARE A flower. Farmers plant seeds to watch you bloom, and as years go by, you grow strong and pretty. Through your years of ups and downs, weather changing with the seasons, the sun has shone, and the rain has fallen, but still you stand tall. Your body figure grows, from a bud to a rose. Now, many bugs land, but only one bee can claim your pollen. Now that you have grown, you can stand on your own roots and take whatever comes your way because you are a flower and flowers bloom. You don't need much in life, only cool shade to keep harmful things away, a little water for continuous growth, and someone to plant some seed for fertilization. You can't just let this beautiful flower grow out here all alone without producing some offspring, now can you? The last ingredient that you need to make this flower complete is some tender loving care to stay moist, hydrated in all the right areas, and protected from gardeners who will try to pluck you by the roots. Instead of helping you grow, they see you withering and will allow you to die right in their own yards: burying your heart and soul. You see, they try to cultivate you by MAKING you grow the way they see fit, but no one can make you do anything you don't want to do. Why? Because it's all up to you to elevate your petals, leaves, and fly high with the birds and the bees. You just need the help of the wind beneath your wings. Will you allow the air to be and respect you. YOU ARE A FLOWER.

The man carries the seed and the woman carries the egg. What a man speaks into a woman she will eventually birth. If it's positive, she becomes an elegant and graceful queen, who exudes confidence. She feels his support and not only wants to serve him in excellence, but also the world. If a man speaks negativity into a woman, she begins to birth resentment, anger, bitterness, sadness, despair, stress, and insecurities. As much as I would stand my ground, argue, and disrespect the one that was disrespecting me, I never fully believed I was everything he said I was. Something inside of me knew it just wasn't true. My spirit wouldn't accept the lies because my mother always told me I was the prize.

I saw him as an individual with a broken past, unhealed wounds, and scar tissue that he had carried around for many years. Jumping from relationship to relationship, procreating with women he thought were the problem. By the time he got to me, he was still yelling at his past. "This dude is crazy," I thought, and then the voices in my head would say, "And you're crazier for staying." I was functioning in my dysfunction. I would seek peace, but couldn't fully receive it because I was deeply involved in a soul tie I knew I had no business in. I would fight off every temptation of really and truly leaving an unhealthy situation. I would come up with excuses: I don't want to break up our family, our children would be heartbroken, who's going to take care of him like me? What would people think? I didn't want the negative stigma that comes with divorce. I was the air he breathed, and he would suffocate without me. I saw some progress. Wasn't that good enough? "At least he's trying," I would say to myself, but he had triggers. He would go off on emotional tangents that were dangerous for our kids and myself. My kids were growing and so was I. I didn't want them to see a poor example of a husband or father. More importantly, I didn't want them to see their mother as a helpless wife. I wanted better for them and better for myself. He didn't support us financially, emotionally, or spiritually and many times he was physically present in the house, but wasn't fully present. I would run laps around him, assisting with homework, projects, and extracurricular activities for the kids to keep them in oblivion. He was, without a doubt, religious and even manipulated me into believing I was doing Satan's work if I gave up on my marriage, which already felt like hell. This man grew up in church, came from a family that was a part of the church, but he didn't act like the church. The church I read wasn't a building, but the body of Christ. A body of believers who follow the example of the kind of life Christ lived and walked while on earth. A walk of love, forgiveness, grace, mercy, kindness, selflessness, power, meekness, and the list could go on and on. What I experienced was the "body of ego," and my own ego used the scripture, "Obedience is better than sacrifice." I was able to talk myself into being obedient to the word of God and not divorcing by sacrificing my marriage. I was allowing stones to be thrown at me and it felt like I was being crucified. I started to feel trapped and I needed a way out. The ball was in my court because the house and bills were in my name and I was paying for it big time. Not only did it cost me financially, it cost me emotionally; I was mentally exhausted.

Comfort is the enemy of success. I was led astray by a false sense of security and I had to get vigilant. It was time for me to fight for my life like it depended on it and it did. I only had one life to live, and I was giving it to someone who didn't deserve it. My life was being interrupted. A shift was taking place and instead of being stagnant, I decided to trust the transformative changes happening inside of me, in order to change my world around me.

My seeds, my daughters, were growing quickly and although I was in a toxic situation, I knew they chose me. They chose me to be their mother, and even though they believe I'm their hero and I saved them, the truth is they're my heroes and they saved my life. Before these two precious seeds, my life didn't have much meaning. Whatever

I was doing was for recognition, acceptance from society, and to be seen on the scene. When they came into my life, my attitude went from vanity to service. I was starting to use my

seeds for growth, through every transition, emotion, season, and change. They were my mirrors showing me who I was.

At times, I was a caterpillar transitioning into a beautiful butterfly. Other times, I was Leo the lion yelling, "Hear me roar" because my passion for them to soar was deep in my soul. At the end of the day, I realized what a miraculous thing I'd done by creating life — human beings, so delicate and complex, precious, and pure, who light up my sometimes-dark world. As I grew, they grew. If I withered, they would too. I told myself, "Rise Keri. You must be resilient. They're depending on you." Our children are gifts from God. Beyond a shadow of doubt, their innocence and free loving spirits come from heaven above, untainted by the pressures of the world or this thing called life. They are so free that they are able to remind the trapped, caged, lost, weak, and confused, to be bold, courageous, and strong, and to realize it's okay to just be — be free. They don't worry about the past or fear the future. They know how to be here, now, and enjoy the moment. My children were teachers for me. They knew how to be happy with simple things and had the kind of childlike faith human beings need in order to love, forgive, and never give up hope. Like the rapper Talib Kweli once said in his song, "Love Language,"

You know a flower that grow in the ghetto
Know more about survival than the one from fresh meadows
It got love for the sun, that's where I'm comin' from

I truly believe children are children of light. They carry the light that was deposited in them from the beginning of time and will continue to carry that light until taught otherwise.

2

Life Interrupted
DOES NOT MEAN LIFE ENDED...

MARRIAGE IS NOT for the weak or faint of heart. It's also not for two broken individuals who are trying to make each other whole. It is often the reflection of things you don't want to see when looking at your partner, that are the things we need to change inevitably. Soulmates are two healthy, whole, individuals that are a blessing to the world. Opposites do actually attract. What is strength for one, could be a weakness in the other. Two positives don't create sparks. A positive and negative do.

Although, I made the mistake of marrying the wrong person and not paying attention to the warning signs, I've honestly learned a lot about myself and relationships. The wisdom I've gained from this experience is priceless, which is why I must share it with you. There were times when we would lash out at one another, but the person we were really talking to was the person on the inside of us. It can be downright ugly and dark at times. Other times, it feels like a euphoric high. It's a love drug and you become addicted to the joy and pain. "But, I thought love should never hurt?" you say. The reality is that hurt people, hurt other people, and if you're a hurting person, it's best to seek help for healing, so you won't bring that baggage into another relationship. It's unfortunate when a person jumps from relationship to relationship without fully processing what went wrong and what went right. People remain who they are, not knowing the problem wasn't with the ex they left. The problem was with themselves. These kinds of people often blame others for their own mistakes or the ending of the relationship. There is no accountability when we can't take a long hard look at ourselves and realize when we're wrong and wonder why our relationships are failing. No matter how different your new someone appears to be from the last person you were in a relationship with, you will always have the same kind of issues you had before because you carry them with you. It is important for people to realize and recognize they are carrying baggage from their past. The new girlfriend, boyfriend, or spouse may start to feel like a punching bag, and to be honest, there is nothing they can say or do to make the relationship better. Each person has a responsibility to want to better themselves, not just for their significant other, but for their own personal growth and healing. Healthy couples have to pick and choose their battles, but don't let the battles of the past or fear of the future pick you. There are some arguments that happen because of what we played out in our minds that never really happened. I remember countless arguments based on a thought process of what could have happened instead of having a conversation about what was actually happening. Oftentimes, we get caught up in what was or what could be, but the real power in love lies in what's happening right now.

Fair Fighting.

HE SPENT SO much time defending positions instead of playing positions. If I would confront a situation, I would hear a million excuses, or my voice would get shut down with "I don't want to hear that shit!" The more time passed, the more comfortable he became in allowing me to play the two roles of husband and wife, nurturer, and provider. I said to myself, "I'm part of the problem. I've enabled this type of behavior for so long, hoping he would change." I thought if I held him down and was his ride or die, he would eventually be motivated to do more to help our circumstances. He didn't mind me struggling because he was reaping the benefits of my hustle. He didn't mind me getting up early every morning to get the kids ready for school, drive us around town, and go to work because it meant that he didn't have to. I once heard a pastor say, "Wives should speak to the king in their husband if they want a king to manifest." My problem was that I tried speaking to a man who didn't realize he was a king. His ego and the women from his past had told him he was one, but the man presented to me was more the fool. Sadly, I found myself speaking to the fool while portraying him to the world as a king. I was more ashamed of myself than him because I knew better. I was attractive, educated, and came from a single mother who didn't take crap from any man. My mother also worked hard to make sure her children didn't want for anything. I followed in her footsteps, but not completely. I had her work ethic, grace, and style, but I lacked wisdom when it came to men because I had the need for validation. There are so many women who believe it's their job to stay in an unhealthy marriage because it's their wifely duty. We become inundated with the idea that it's our responsibility to love him back to who he should be, but that man has got to *want* to be a better version of himself!

One day, and I remember it so clearly, God told me to "Let go."

"Huh? Let go of what, God?" There was so much hidden anger, resentment, and bitterness on the inside of me, I wasn't sure if the instructions were to let go of the unhealthy emotions or to let go of him. I didn't realize I was drinking the poison of those feelings because I suppressed them for so long in order to take care of business as usual. I was numb to the pain, used to the shame, and expected disappointment because that's who we were.

"Let Go." I heard it time and time again, but never thought it meant let go of this marriage. Life as I knew it for the past decade was being interrupted. God hates divorce, right? Religion had me bound. As spiritual as I thought I was, I couldn't dare divorce him. I thought I was being punished so I sought counseling. I first sought counseling alone, to be clear about what God was telling me to do. Then I sought counseling for us as a couple and soon realized you're only going to get out of counseling what you put in it. We had homework to do. I wanted my marriage to work no matter what, so I would do the assignments, put in the practical work, and take action. I would walk past his booklet and open it up, only to see blank pages. I was disappointed in the minimal efforts, and it led me to believe he wasn't interested in fighting for this marriage. He was more interested in holding on to his security blanket. In his mind, there wasn't a problem, and nothing needed to be fixed because he was on the taking end of our marriage, while I was on the giving side. At the end of the day, he didn't just take my finances, resources, or body, he took all of my energy. I felt like I had no other choice but to bury myself in busy work to suppress what was really going on inside of me. I was unhappy and knew that I deserved so much more than what I was getting, and my children did too. I started loving me more, more than he thought he did. I was getting stronger, more courageous, and brave enough to understand God hadn't made my shoulders to carry so many heavy burdens. I started to emotionally check out, realizing a physical check out was coming soon. I started to stretch—not in the physical aspect—but in a way that every part of my soul was shifting from weakness to strength. I began to realize what he called love was really just dependency. Then, life whispered, "This can't be love." My life was being interrupted and I had to see my value the same way my creator did.

~The Beauty of a Woman~

The beauty of a woman is not in the clothes she wears,
The figure she carries, or the way she combs her hair.
The beauty of a woman must be seen from her eyes,
Because that is the doorway to her heart,
The place where love resides.
The beauty of a woman is not in a facial mole,
But true beauty in a woman is reflected in her soul.
It is the caring that she lovingly gives,
The passion that she shows.
The beauty of a woman
With passing years — only grows.
—Audrey Hepburn

On May 1st, 2016, a few days before our wedding anniversary, I told myself, "I'm leaving him."

He asked me, "What do you want to do this year for our anniversary?"

I'm thinking, "Well, here we go again, I have to plan and pay for our date." I wasn't up for an anniversary that year because I had many financial responsibilities to take care of. Additionally, I wanted to feel like someone was finally planning and paying for a date for me. I was tired of playing that role. I was providing for our family, trying to protect us from hurt, harm, and danger. I was careful about who I let in our home, but he wasn't. There were all kinds of people he brought around that served no purpose in our lives. We are only as good as the company we keep, and although I didn't pass judgement on the type of people he brought around, I didn't understand why he hung out with them. None of them were in positions to help him, inspire him, or challenge him to grow. As much as I knew these people didn't wish him harm, they also didn't wish him well and if I brought it up he would become defensive. So, I left it alone and dealt with the fact that this is who he was and who he wanted to be. I couldn't say much because I was trying to escape our reality, which was going nowhere fast. I didn't want to argue either. I was more than tired; I was exhausted.

Each morning he would wake up on the wrong side of the bed and I immediately felt his negative energy. This was one of many typical distractions. My focus was taken away from all the good the universe was bringing into my life. Instead, I was focused on what he lacked, his coldness, instability, and selfishness. I was witnessing a little boy trapped inside a man's body, going through the same cycles over and over again, while throwing temper tantrums to reel me back in. It was all drama and chaos on an emotional roller coaster. Life could have been so simple, but I knew it would continue in this cycle until he committed another petty crime. Yes, unfortunately, my children were exposed to seeing their father in handcuffs, or hearing that someone from law enforcement was looking for him in order to serve a warrant for his arrest. They saw this quite often, as it would happen almost every year. I could no longer protect his image to them. They saw for themselves that daddy had done something wrong and had to suffer the consequences. I've always tried to teach them about right and wrong and how there are laws in this world put in place for society to follow. If we break the law, we will pay for it. The next time he went to jail it felt different for me. I wasn't concerned about what would happen to him, whereas before, I would cry and lose sleep. This time my attitude was like, "Fuck it!"

The neighbors were talking and gossiping endlessly about what caused him to go to jail. It got to the point that whenever I would pull into my driveway they would look the other way with guilt written on their faces. One even called me personally to tell me she'd called the police on him. I later found out the motive behind her reasoning. There had been some inappropriate behavior between the two of them and they had me looking foolish. I was angry at both of them, but didn't seek to take matters into my own hands until she involved my children. This was a woman I trusted to watch my kids, and she had the nerve to try and punish them by calling the homeowners association in an attempt to have us banned from using the common areas, such as the park, tennis courts, and pool. At that point I was ready to hurt her. I acted out of character and thankfully I didn't go to jail, I finally realized the sweetest revenge was for me to move forward without looking back. The man that I tried to portray as a great father and husband to the outside world had finally been exposed as the man he really was, and I didn't care to protect his image or mine, because I knew this was a pivotal moment for me, as I was closing on my new home. I was getting ready to leave him and all the drama behind. My focus shifted, and I was proud of myself. This time, I let go of him for real! My realtor called me and said "Congratulations, Keri, you're closing on your new home!" My life was being interrupted and my soul was transcending towards the spirit it was created to be. While I was rebuilding my mind, heart, and soul from the inside out, I was also in the beginning phases of building a house from the ground up. When I got serious about leaving the drama behind, the universe responded and got serious about me! It was time to truly let go and let God.

3

Life Interrupted:
NEW BEGINNINGS

Full of gratefulness, as I made color selections in my new home, God strategically placed the right realtor, agent, and builder in my life. As my home was taking shape and form, brick by brick, my spirit was willing to go higher, level after level. I was on a journey and it was more than physical; it was spiritual. The holy spirit will not force itself upon you, it will only come when you're ready. Its voice is as loud as our willingness to listen. I was willing to listen because the things I'd been listening to were not working for me and were so far off from the truth. God is a God of many chances and He was giving me a chance to start over again. I was transforming and transitioning at the same time. Although, I was starting over, I felt brave. I finally had peace. The kind that really surpasses all understanding. I didn't understand why my marriage was dissolving and why I didn't get the "happily ever after." I couldn't process why my children had to be in the middle of that cross fire. Then one day my "why" shifted to "what," and I found my answer by asking the question, "What is the lesson and purpose in this God?" I never wanted my marriage to fail, but I understood clearly that it was time to move on. Into the unknown, I fearlessly stayed close to the creator and it felt like angels were rejoicing all around me.

Doors were opening, and heaven was on my side, but I realized I had to be stronger than ever because there was so much on the line. For our children, my most prized possessions, I had to show resilience, so I never let them see me sweat. I couldn't show them I was a little afraid, I saved my tears for my closet and in that same place is where I would go to war. Praying on my knees, strategically aligning with God on how to move forward. When it was time to be transparent, I was vulnerable and open to them. Vulnerability was not a sign of weakness, it was a strength that humbled me in order to be transparent. I let my children know that I was wounded, but not broken and that we would get through it. I was sure of who I was and wanted them to know they inspired me to get there. I never wanted them to carry the burdens for a man that should have carried for his family. It didn't feel okay and it was not okay. I signed my daughters up for counseling because their lives were essentially interrupted. Life as they knew it changed dramatically. They were used to a two-parent household and now had to live with one. They wanted mommy and daddy back together without understanding how unhappy I was. I tried my best to explain to them how much we loved them, and the separation wasn't their fault. The counselor gave them vivid examples of how we were still a family, and that it was only the dynamics that had changed, but my daughters were hurt. I flashed back to the pain of my father having to leave our home as I agonized in tears asking my mother, "Why?" She couldn't respond verbally, so she responded physically by holding me tighter. My mind went from the feelings in that memory to how I felt throughout my adolescent, teen, and young adult years. I told myself, "I got through it and so will they." I then felt like a failure because for so long I had vowed to not end up the way my parents had, and there I was going down a similar path. There were many times I felt embarrassed and ashamed and no one knew my struggles or pain. No one, that is, except my mother. As much as I would protect this man from anyone's judgement, by not telling a soul of what really went on behind closed doors, my mother's intuition and discernment were more powerful than my secrets. What would people think or say if they really knew the truth? I had to come to a place of acceptance. Accepting all that was and all that could be if I didn't concern myself with the opinions of others. Those that really mattered would understand and those that didn't understand didn't have to. There was a lion inside of me that finally needed to roar for herself and not for others.

~Keri The Lion~

The others are trying to manifest my

Extravagant, exuberant, and inherent

Ability

To shine and radiate

Naturally, like the sun…

Only a ruby can compliment my

Grace and fill my

Empty space with

Serenity

My smile illuminates

Like gold, my body is a

Perfect subject

To mold and sculpt

To be forever etched in time like a precious

Artifact

In da zodiac I

Rule the spine, heart, and

The back

Making my back

The location of

Pleasure

And my heart the location

Of my deepest treasure....

Leo is my zodiac sign

Keri the Lion is really divine

Although, I was leaving a toxic situation, it still took some time for me to get rid of the words that were spoken to me because they were embedded in my mind. I was believing and carrying lies about me, which men of similar qualities picked up on immediately. I didn't know the energy I put off into the universe was one that could be picked up on by strangers. The type of men that approached me had similar character traits to his. Some of them even had his swag with tattoos, ball caps, and oversized clothes. They were attracted to a woman who still wasn't sure of herself on the inside, but exuded confidence on the outside. I made sure my hair and nails were intact, my eyebrows, lashes, and lipstick (my must-have makeup trinity) were flawless, and my outfits of choice were unique, so I stood out. My smile was just about the only thing that I didn't put much effort into because it was effortless. No matter what I had been through, no matter how many things he tried to steal, my smile that was the one thing that never left me. I had to get free and heal for my daughters, as well as the people in the world God wanted me to serve. My purpose was bigger than this tainted love. My life was being interrupted for a purpose bigger than me.

Art is imitating life. No question. All of these broken-hearted stories are real. We live them every day. All of these pretty pictures we paint in our heads aren't what we're living, which is why they're imagined in the first place. We want to escape our realities, so we dream, but we are in our own way, so we don't fully realize the dream can come true. It's like the matrix, what you see, is not what you get. We're afraid to create another love story through our art (hearts) by choosing the wrong person again. So, in the meantime, we keep being artists, painting beautiful pictures of our spouses, children, homes, cars, and careers, while not doing the necessary work to heal ourselves in order to make those dreams a reality.

Master MANipulator

MY LOVE FOR God was used against me. While peace, love, and joy grew in me, the change I needed and wanted desperately to see was actually starting to happen. While I loved him with every ounce of my being, there was a higher level of consciousness in me that wouldn't let me settle or walk in his shadow any longer. There had been times when I finally stopped fearing leaving, but his charismatic, slick, poetic, words would soften my heart that was building walls he tried to break down. I would go back to believing his words, "that nobody is going to love you as much as I do." He mistook arrogance for confidence quite often, and I almost got sucked back into the twilight zone. I had to shift my focus towards building my new home. I started thanking the enemy of my soul for every test and trial, bringing me to my knees and pushing me closer to my destiny. Whoever said, "Keep your friends close and your enemies closer," knew what they were talking about. He was the best enemy I ever had, teaching me my greatest life lesson: Self-love. If he hadn't loved me the wrong way, I may have never known to love me the right way. My life was interrupted. This didn't start when I married him. This was years of me allowing emotionally, unavailable, unstable men to choose me because that is what I was accustomed to. It was time for me to take full responsibility for my actions and to get to the root cause of my behaviors in order for me to better myself.

My father left us for the streets when I was eleven years old. As my single mother worked two jobs to provide for my brother and myself, I started taking care of my eight-year-old brother while our mother worked her night job. I thought I was teaching him how to be tough, by fighting him and protecting him from outsiders, while making sure he kept all my secrets. The need to save and take care of a male began right there. I was only eleven years old and since I couldn't save my father, I did the next best thing, by doing everything in my power to try and save my brother. Most of my male family members were either in prison, sold drugs, or had been slain in the streets, so anything opposite of that lifestyle was abnormal to me. Once I realized that the root causes of my issues were my past influences and a lack of self-love, I began to make wiser choices when it came to men and that's when the healing process began. Now, healing isn't an overnight process, it's often like an onion that gets peeled off, layers by layer. I was on the road to recovery and wholeness. Now that I was in this place, it was imperative that I didn't go back to brokenness. Like the addict in recovery can relapse, so can we if we're not careful and paying attention to what causes certain things and how they affect us in relationships. When you're trying to get to the other side of the wall, there are walls on the inside of you that must come down first in order to open your heart to true love. There will be a process of changing from one state into another. Embrace your life being interrupted because it will take you to the next level. You must get comfortable being uncomfortable. The world wants you to believe that hardening your heart will allow you to never get hurt again. The reality is, not opening your heart to love again is far more dangerous. You will lose your senses, and as human beings, we were all created to give and receive love. Without it, we're not really alive.

Confirmation

I DIDN'T KNOW my own strength. It was a typical Sunday morning and church had just let out. I was still "drunk in the spirit," as church folks would say, which basically means that I was on a natural high, feeling more connected to God than ever before. The love and joy in my heart were radiating through my bright eyes, as I was fellowshipping with a few saints. There was a judge running for office, who was visiting our church. She saw my smile from across the room and said, "You are beautiful. If people can't see your spirit, there's a problem with them, not you." Oh my God! I needed to hear those words. Getting ready for church that morning, my husband had said the exact opposite. Regardless, if he didn't see my beauty and value, someone else did. It was the confirmation I needed to know that my life and purpose was bigger than what I could see, or what this man had been saying to me for years, and that was, "You're not worth it." I was able to find peace in a house full of pain. When you're with a man that invests so little into your being, you reap little benefits. It was time for me to get out and never apologize for adjusting the crown I was meant to wear. I started finding and seeing the good in everyone. Even him. I tried to find common ground and understanding, to put myself in his shoes in order to figure out why he operated the way he did. I'm not playing victim here and I take full responsibility for my enabling actions. Our jobs are to exercise forgiveness and mercy towards ourselves and others in order to move on from what was and to accept what will be. We're more alike than different. Let love continue to drive you and be the most powerful voice in your life. Let it be heard over all the pain and strife. Don't you dare suffer a day longer. If your mate doesn't want to rise to the occasion, let them lay low and lay alone. You're too valuable to suffer the consequences of settling. Your life needs to be interrupted and often times it comes with confirmation from people, places, and things that we either chose to listen to, or ignore.

The Naked Truth

A MAN WITH no vision has no direction. I let him feel like he was taking the lead as a man, but mentally, physically, spiritually, and emotionally it ended up being my job. It was exhausting playing two roles, when I was created to only play one. One of my roles, was to step up as the man in the relationship by being the breadwinner, making provisions for our children, and protecting our daughters by any means necessary. The other role, was trying my best to be nurturing as a woman and mother. I thank God for his grace as I look back over my life. I still don't know how I got it done. You never know how strong you are until you have to be. The truth was, I told myself I would not be another one of his bitter baby momma's, so I put myself on a pedestal and told myself we were married. I didn't come up with this "marriage thing" alone. We made vows in my apartment as husband and wife, so in my mind we were married. I later realized that this was only a game he played in order to get what he wanted. After investing in pre-marital counseling and becoming pregnant with our first child, I was determined to not allow him to get off the hook so easily and was determined to marry him. In the midst of some of his family members being jealous of our relationship, as well as his baby momma and ex-wife, we began to feel like we were against all odds. The rebel in the both of us told us we had something to prove, so we did. We got married in the midst of all the drama and red flags. It was him and me against the world, and for every failed past relationship he'd had, I told myself it would be better with me because I was different. He wouldn't treat me the way he treated them because he didn't really love them, he loved me. He wouldn't womanize me or allow me to take care of him because he truly cared about me. But the truth is, old habits die hard. Be careful to say what you would never do. I mocked the women in his past, calling them stupid sugar mommas with low self-esteem. And while he did morph slightly outside of his comfort zone, loving me in a way he never loved before, it still didn't stop me from playing a familiar role he and I had both seen before. I couldn't believe I was displaying some of the same behaviors I said I would never exhibit, and that truth really hurt.

There's Beauty in Your Brokenness

YOU MADE A mistake, but you are not the mistake you made. When we walk around believing we are what we did, we forget who we are, and the power in our lives shifts from what we were created to be, into what we think we should be. Too often we are walking around in shame, disappointment, resentment, hurt, bitterness, and the list could go on and on. Shame is an enemy of confidence. Leave because you want to leave; because wanting to leave is enough. This doesn't just pertain to relationships. This pertains to all aspects of life, from career, family, friends, and anything that no longer serves you. It took me a while to learn that "No" is a complete sentence. Stop trying to explain yourself to anyone who doesn't add value to your life. I had to stop trying to please everyone and realize I had nothing to prove and only one to please. As long as God was happy and guiding me towards abundance, so was I. Not everyone is going to understand your reasoning, and they shouldn't. God didn't speak my next move to them, he spoke it to me. That came with some casualties of war. I lost the man I gave my heart to and devoted my life to, but what I gained was priceless. I knew there had to be something greater for me on the other side of the wall.

If I could just knock it down, perhaps climb over it, and get a preview or a glimpse of what it was, I would have the strength to keep going. I wanted to persevere in the midst of trials and things happening beyond my control because I wanted so desperately to see my end from the beginning. I had to picture myself winning. Day by day, something inside of me gave me permission to keep going. The spirit inside of me was warring with everything around me that told me to go back, to stay where I was because the road ahead was too difficult to face alone. I chose to listen to one voice and one voice only. I got really still and quiet, prayed a lot, and stayed as close to God as I could for more wisdom, direction, insight, and clarity. There were many voices around me, including his persuasive "Don't leave me" arguments. There were friends and family members that I trusted to tell my plans to and to pray for my daughters and me. Some of them had the best intentions by telling me to "work it out," but they had no idea that I couldn't listen to their voices. God was in me and all around me and He knew what was best. I trusted the spirit of God with my entire life and He had chosen to interrupt it. If the creator of this world showed us our futures in the present time, many of us would stop trying to get to the other side. We would miss out on some of life's most important lessons: perseverance, strength, courage, wisdom, love, joy, and peace. We would either be afraid of what was on the other side of the wall, or we would lose our will to do whatever was required to get there. Anything worth having is not easy to get. Our fortitude and integrity would be weakened because we didn't have enough faith, strength, or courage to pursue the victories laying ahead. Our creator gave us everything we need on the inside to accomplish the things He created us to do. In order to do this, we must clear our clouded minds in order for the soul to shout. We must allow our lives to be interrupted. In my most private moments alone with God, I would receive clarity, direction, and wisdom for each day.

"For without me ye can do nothing." (John 15:5 KJV)

Whenever I tried to do something without the guidance of the Holy Spirit it was exhausting. I was operating outside of grace and trying to fit God into my life plans, when I should have been following the plans God had for my life instead. There wasn't a single time in my adult life where I made a decision and didn't know if it was right or wrong. I'm not talking about being at a crossroad and having to make a decision that could change the course of my life. I'm referring to those moments when I was approached with something that didn't feel right to my psyche, but I went with it because my weakened state of mine wanted it. No matter the cost, I took a chance. The rebel in me thought I could handle whatever came my way, however, some of my encounters were absolutely life threatening, and when I look back over my life it's a miracle that I'm still alive. Thank God for interrupting my soul.

4

Life Interrupted:
OUR EXPERIENCES SHAPE US.

I RECALL A TIME when I believed that due to my own experiences, of dealing with the men in my family who were broken, in prison, selling drugs, robbing, and falling victim to the streets, that I could save anyone who walked a similar path. I honestly believed that there was beauty in their brokenness, and God could use me to work miracles in their lives. There was, however, one catch. They had to want the miracle for themselves as well. Although this wasn't a bad concept, to save the lost and broken-hearted, it was an unwise decision when you consider the fact that I wasn't listening to the guidance and direction of the miracle worker Himself. After all, God is where your protection lies.

During this time, my only blood brother was sentenced to seven years in prison for armed robbery, my dad was somewhere on the streets, and the void I was so desperately trying to fill, was one that sought love and acceptance, especially from men. I was around the age of twenty-three and working at a gym as a personal trainer and assistant manager, when one of the guys at the car wash, which was located on our property, took a liking to me. It was my genuine smile, angelic personality, and non-judgmental approach to people that attracted most men to me. I treated everyone the same, no matter their position or title. This guy seemed a little shy, but looked physically strong. Truth be told, he had a beautiful physique. After his shift, he would come into the gym to work out, and I couldn't help but notice him staring at me from across the room. When he let me know his interest in me, I was hesitant because he worked outside of my job at the carwash we owned, and I never mixed business with pleasure. I always wanted to keep the two separate. Despite my initial uncertainty, I took a chance, but it wasn't long before I learned, through mutual people we knew, that he wasn't quite the man he said he was.

One time in particular, I was shopping around for car insurance at a place he had referred me to, and when he stepped outside, the sales lady, who just happened to be one of my high school classmates, took the opportunity to give me a warning that I was shocked to hear. She told me how he brutally beat the mother of his child and to stay away from his entire family. She claimed they were a family full of violent brothers that lived lives of crime. That warning had me leery, but I wasn't afraid enough to leave him alone.

I met his mother, who seemed genuine at the time and his young daughters, who were around the ages of five and six years old. The older daughter, who lived with his mother, gravitated towards my youthful personality immediately. I recognized her as a beautiful, broken soul too. I learned her mother had left her at a very young age, and due to her father's run-ins with the law, her grandmother had full custody of her and she was just happy to be in the presence of a young woman because she so desperately wanted what other little girls her age had, a mother. Whenever I would visit, her face lit up. I thought to myself, "I don't mind taking on this 'mother figure' role. After all, she's a sweet, beautiful little girl."

As our relationship deepened, her father wanted some alone time with me and because the house didn't allow for much privacy, with his mother and daughter there, he took me to his brother's apartment, which I later found out was an apartment community for the mentally ill. His brother mainly stayed with his girlfriend, who was also mentally ill and lived in the apartment next door. It took a little while, but eventually I became comfortable enough to start spending the night there. One morning, I remember getting up to get ready for work, but he didn't want me to leave. I told him I was going to be late for work and to please let me go. All of a sudden, he turned into a person I had never seen before. He was holding me against my will, and I didn't know how to get free. I was being held hostage at gunpoint, and when I finally figured out a way to escape, I yelled "HELP" and ran from the apartment to my car. Somehow, I got inside my jeep quickly enough to roll my windows up and lock the doors. I screeched out of the parking lot and headed to work as I cried hysterically and tried to get myself together to train clients for the day. My mind went back to the day my classmate tried to warn me about his abusive behavior. She'd been right, and I told myself to stay away from him.

The next encounter I had with him, he asked if I could give him a ride home to his mother's house. My naive, forgiving nature caused me to be in denial of what this man was truly capable of, and I allowed him to be in my presence again. I don't remember how the conversation went, but I do remember him making me drive in the opposite direction of his mother's house. It was a set up. As soon as I realized he was looking for a secluded place to put his hands on me, I started paying attention to my surroundings. I saw a church with people standing around it and I thought that if I could just get out of the car and yell for help I wouldn't be another victim! The opportunity presented itself as the light was changing from yellow to red. I slowed down, grabbed the keys out of the ignition, and jumped out the moving vehicle. Screaming frantically, I headed toward the people at the church. Luckily, they saw me running across the street, yelling hysterically, and not paying attention to oncoming traffic. When I reached the group, breathing heavily, I tried to get the words out "Call the police."

He was, of course, watching from across the street and decided to run just in case the cops showed up. That was twice I'd escaped physical harm, but the damage was done mentally. I knew God had angels around me because I was able to escape those hostile situations. I also knew he had a plan for my life as I lived through it. What I didn't understand was why I chose to allow this type of person in my life and why these types of people gravitated towards me. I was damaged and didn't know it. I couldn't see it then, but my life was being interrupted and because I didn't want the disruption, I continued to suffer.

While I was in college, I dated like-minded individuals that were young, impressionable, seeking higher education, and wanted to make something of their lives just like I did. I met my college sweetheart my sophomore year and we remained in a committed relationship until my senior year. I decided to break up with him that year because I believed he was too nice and was becoming too attached. The reality was he just loved me the way I should have been loved, but because I never knew a love like this I pushed him away. I'd done the same thing in high school with my high school sweetheart only I didn't notice the trend. I thought I became bored after a few years of commitment and the relationship just wasn't meant to be.

When I moved back to my hometown after college, I chose to date "bad guys." They were men whose backgrounds contained felonies and little education. They sold drugs and were generally emotionally unavailable. I chose them because of the challenges they presented. I didn't have enough drama in my life, so I allowed them to create it in mine. I also didn't believe I was worthy of love. I believed I could give it, but didn't want to fully receive it. I was afraid because I had abandonment issues. If I could partner with someone that claimed they loved me, but didn't show it to me, it wouldn't hurt as much if they were to ever leave. Furthermore, there was never a dull moment and I wouldn't become bored.

The men I chose, however, weren't the problem — I was. I chose men with similar patterns from my past and character traits that I was accustomed to. They were men that would possibly leave me and weren't fully available. These were open wounds that I hadn't allowed to heal, which caused me to make illogical decisions. I wanted to be in control by allowing unhealthy relationships in my life to exist, so when the time came for the relationship to end, I could blame the other party, even though I was the irresponsible one. I had an unhealthy thought process, and it was time for something to happen in my life that would change the outlook I had on myself and the type of men I allowed to come into it. There comes a time when your life is interrupted with something so traumatic that the course changes forever. What you choose to do in those moments is critical to your journey. Life interrupted becomes a testimony.

T.D. WAS THE first friend I met when I moved to Atlanta, GA. Although her life at the time appeared to be young, wild, and free she had the heart of an angel.

T.D was the kind of friend that you didn't judge, no matter how she chose to live her life, because she truly cared for people. To know her was to love her, and those that didn't know her only saw what manifested on the outside. She appeared to be a party girl, looking for love in the all the wrong places, and attracting the kind of men who were abusive, disrespectful, and demeaning toward women. T.D. would also entertain men that could offer her lavish gifts. Some would call it gold digging.

One day, T.D. and I were heading to the grocery store when a guy that most women would call "fine," was walking down the street. T.D was bold enough to approach him and ask for his number. In that moment I did judge her because I never had the audacity to approach a guy, but T.D always went after what she wanted, and generally got it. She was ecstatic after she got his number and said, "Oh my God. I finally got me somebody." I felt awkward because I didn't know what to say, but I remember thinking to myself, "Some women don't know how to be alone." I left Atlanta after becoming pregnant with my second child, but still kept in touch with T.D from my hometown in Florida. When I moved back to Atlanta, eight months after my youngest was born, I invited T.D and some other friends over for a get together at my house. When I saw her again, something was noticeably different. She wasn't drinking alcohol or smoking weed. She started telling me about this African man she'd met that she was in love with. I didn't think much about it, but the next conversation we had was one about her giving her life to Christ. "Wow!" I thought to myself. "She quit everything cold turkey." I was astonished with her life interrupting. She did a complete 360 and changed dramatically. She would no longer listen to secular music, go to the club, date multiple men, drink alcohol, or smoke weed. She was a new person, comfortable in her own skin and with her own decisions.

T.D later told me she was married to the African guy she was enamored with, and I was extremely happy for my friend, but her new life came with some challenges. She lost some friends along the way that wanted her to remain the same. Beyond that, the new love of her life was facing deportation back to Africa after being arrested in Georgia for a petty crime. Through these challenges, T.D's faith increased all the more. She prayed and trusted God with her whole heart and was crazy enough to consider moving to Africa if her husband was deported. Love is powerful. Thankfully, he was released after a year and they continued their lives together in the United States. T.D. used to say that she would never have any more children, but when she met her husband she wanted a child with him. Her tubes had been clipped, burnt, and tied after her last child, so this was going to take a miracle. Despite the challenge, T.D. and her husband continued to plan for a family. They were excited to find out she was pregnant, but a few months later they lost the baby and later found out there was another one inside that needed to be removed. They were heartbroken, but that didn't stop their faith. T.D. was resilient and determined to trust God for a child, specifically a baby girl after having two sons already. Another year past and T.D was pregnant again. This time, fear edged its way into the happiness and when she called me to pray with her, I gladly did. Thirty-five weeks later, T.D. and her husband introduced their miracle baby, Ami, to the world and it gave me inspiration. Inspiration to believe in second chances, to not doubt the power of God, and to know that true love still exists. My heart was encouraged to believe in the power of God and his miracles.

It's important to position yourself in preparation for what you really want. T.D didn't wait until all the right conditions were met in order to find love again and have a child. She began preparing for her future the moment she realized she had to change within in order for the world to change around her. Often times, we want the blessing, but not the process. Transformation is absolutely necessary to prepare us for our best lives. In order to win in life, we must first see ourselves the way God sees us. Once we see ourselves the way God sees us, we can diminish the negative voices we hear in our heads that tell us we're not good enough. We don't have to settle for who we use to be, but instead we can strive towards who we were created to be. After seeing ourselves greater than where we currently are, we can begin speaking into our futures and the lives we desire to live. We have to replace what we've said about ourselves, and let others see the manifestation of our thoughts and words by seizing every opportunity to reinvent ourselves. All it takes is one step at a time by doing what we can. Just start with what you have by getting out of your comfort zone and stretching beyond what you thought was possible. You can actually become the best version of yourself when doing your best is your only option, even when it results in failure. Knowing that you did your best is the only way to win.

5

Life Interrupted:
HEALTH IS WEALTH

As a former athlete and Exercise Science major in college, I thought of myself as fairly health conscious when it came to physical fitness, but I didn't take my eating habits seriously. My metabolism was fast, and my genetics were a gift from God, so I didn't feel the need to put much effort into my physical appearance. Yet, despite my genes, I, like many freshmen on college campuses, gained the freshman fifteen. I barely cooked and my main meals consisted of fast food from the food court. I didn't know how to shop for groceries to prepare meals, but I quickly learned how to do so when I was no longer on the meal plan. When you start running out of money, you quickly figure out how to make meals stretch.

It wasn't until my face started breaking out due to what I was putting into my body that I started to care about what I was eating. As a model on campus, my physical appearance was geared towards vanity and not to be healthy. I was naive and quite self-absorbed until after I graduated college and moved back to my hometown in Jacksonville, FL.

My hometown was quite different from the college town I'd become accustomed to. Jacksonville had a lot of potential, but it also had a selfish mentality born out of segregation. There was the black side of town and the white side of town. A rich side of town and a poor side of town. Somewhere in the middle was the middle class and that is where most of the people I grew up with lived. In a city where crime was high and coming together as a community was low, many people were out for themselves and our city became known for the crabs in a bucket mentality. As soon as one crab tried to break free, another one was pulling it back down inside the bucket to stay with the rest of them that were going nowhere.

I was miles away from my college friends and I missed having them around for girl talk, social activities, and networking. My life consisted of going to work and coming home. So much so, that I eventually found myself hanging around the wrong kind of people while searching for fun. I didn't have time to meet new friends, and I didn't dare go to clubs by myself, so whatever company my brother kept became my company too. The saying "bad company corrupts good morals" was something I was actually living. I was doing things my mother taught me never to do, and I became so reckless that I found myself stressed out, evicted from my apartment, used, and abused. One day, I woke up to a health scare that changed my life forever. It was a defining moment in my life, as well as a moment I agonized over and had a pity party over for a little while. Too ashamed to tell anyone, but my mother what happened, I realized my life was being interrupted. God was trying to tell me, "you're too valuable to not take care of yourself." He was trying to wake me up from being so blinded by the need for someone. He was trying to tell me to stop self-inflicting myself with things and people that could damage my reputation and integrity. God interrupted me by telling me he loved me, and his love was all the love I needed to be whole in my mind, body, and soul. I took my body for granted by playing Russian roulette, thinking I was invincible. I was more concerned with the temporary pleasures of life instead of the permanent consequences. I believed I needed to be liked by everyone because I loved everyone.

When I hit rock bottom everyone I thought was my friend was actually an illusion. They were blood sucking leeches trying to get everything out of me and gave nothing in return. The best thing that could have happened to me was having those people disappear from my life. Whether it was my own actions, or from God removing them without me having to do a thing, I took the chance and moved back into my mother's house to rebuild my life from the ground up. As I broke out in tears she came in the room and comforted me. She knew the people I'd been around were no good for me and had tried to warn me, but I didn't want to listen. Experience was my greatest teacher. At that moment my mother said, "Be wise and selective when choosing friends, especially young men. No one has the power to make you happier than the right one, or more miserable than the wrong one." Those powerful words stuck with me every day and manifested into real life situations as I navigated through right and wrong relationships.

I remember calling one of my best friends to check on her, as she was still in college, one year behind me. She was in so much pain and didn't know what was happening to her body that it saddened me. We later found out, she was suffering from rheumatoid arthritis, which is a debilitating disease that worsens over time. At twenty-one years old, her life was immediately interrupted. She was unable to do the things that she used to, such as walk at a normal pace, climb stairs without feeling pain, or even wear high-heeled shoes. I couldn't imagine what she was going through and I desperately wanted to be there for her. A part of me wished I could have taken her place because in my mind, she didn't deserve this, but I did. My health issues were self-inflicted, where hers were not. She was too good of a person for something like this to happen to her. As the years went by, I noticed her resilience and determination to not let this ailment derail or discourage her from living with purpose. She remained positive, sweet, and kind to everyone she encountered. She smiled daily and never got depressed, no matter how much pain she was in. I admired her so much, as she was one of the strongest people I knew.

Health obstacles don't enter our lives to stifle us, they come to awaken us. Awaken us to learn new lessons and experience challenges that test our weaknesses and strengths. Everyone handles health complications differently, but the healing process always starts in the mind. There is a direct correlation between the way we perceive things to be and the outcome of those things. If we think a health issue will conquer us, it most likely will. We start believing we are the condition of what we were diagnosed with and start to live our lives subpar and defeated. We begin to settle for the physical limitations based on how we look, feel, or what professional physicians have advised us. Our minds are one of the most powerful weapons we could use to refute those notions. Although we have an illness, it doesn't have to determine our futures. Instead, we can live our best lives now, even with limitations, by accepting proper health care and a positive attitude to help overcome and eventually maintain a life that's intentionally fulfilling.

6

Life Interrupted:
STOP DREAMING YOU STOP LIVING

*S*OMETIMES, WE END up going through the motions of reacting to whatever life hands us. We perceive things through a lens of what this world taught us, and it's the furthest thing from the truth. We become robotic, like modern day slaves. We wake up to fulfill our employer's dreams, while neglecting the calling on our lives. We ignore the voice of reason that gives us purpose, and instead listen to the voices around us that tell us do what they want. We buy into the "work for a living" state of mind in order to expect a paycheck on Friday, instead of the "living to work" mentality, which is the legacy we leave behind as our life's work is connected to our destiny. We get the kids ready for school, assist with homework, attend after school activities, and invest in extracurriculars on the side, hoping it will feed our pride and make us feel like we're achieving the American dream. By the end of the work-week and weekend, it's time to do it all over again. The cycle repeats itself and by the time we're at retirement age, we wonder if we really lived at all. There are people that retire and are so unhealthy from the stress they carried throughout the years that they are unable to enjoy it. I don't want to be that person and I don't want you to be that person either, so something has to give and that "something" is you.

You have to give. You have to give more to yourself, your health, your mentality, your finances, and relationships. I'm not saying quit your job, which is the source of our incomes, but I am saying that you should be wise and make use of the time by doing your best for your employer without compromising your integrity. Give them what they need, but give yourself more. We are no good to those we serve if we aren't any good to ourselves. We were all born with something to give to this world that only we can do. Whatever that is, work on it like no tomorrow. With every second of free time you have, give back to yourself. No one is going to invest in you, like you. You can't expect others to treat you better than you do. Who's going to take you seriously, if you don't take yourself seriously? Who's going to love you, if you don't love you? Who's going to be confident in you and your abilities, if you aren't? While most people search outside of themselves for the resources to accomplish their dreams, the real source is on the inside of you. You are a creative, powerful human being, no matter your circumstances! Take the first step towards achieving your goal, which often times is writing the vision. When you see it, you can move towards it. The ideas will come, and the universe will respond by placing the right people and things in your life to help you get to that destination. Don't worry about the 'how." Your job is to focus on the "what." God will take care of the how, and that is when taking a leap of faith comes in. Pursuing your dreams will come with some roadblocks along the way. You have to ask yourself the question, "How bad do I want it?" Will you take a detour? Will you turn around and go the other way? Anything is possible for those who believe. You must figure out a way to go through the problem by seeing the end from the beginning. Don't avoid it, or go around it. Go through it! Once you come out of it, your strength and capabilities grow in order to take you higher. Once you get there, don't stop! Often times, we think "we've arrived" when we get to our promised land and we become complacent and comfortable, which is a dangerous place to be because the soul and spirit long for growth. When you stop growing, you start dying. Don't become the dead amongst the living. Whenever there's an advancement towards your purpose, there will always be a counterattack. Embrace it. It's developing you for your next encounter with purpose. Allow your life to be interrupted!

7

Life Interrupted:
PLANTING, PLOWING, AND GROWING

Every battle begins in the mind. Wars are either won or lost there. The mind is one of the most powerful things God ever gave us. If we think it, then we begin to speak it, and once we say it, our words take form and then we start acting out our thoughts. Not long after that the behaviors start to shape our world that stemmed from our thought process. The mind is strong, yet it is also tricky. Experts estimate that the mind thinks between 60,000 to 80,000 thoughts a day. That's an average of 2500 to 3,300 thoughts per hour. That's incredible. Other experts estimate a smaller number, of 50,000 thoughts per day, which means about 2100 thoughts per hour. This too, is a great number of thoughts. (www.successconsciousness.com). It is critical for us to try and control our thoughts as much as we can, especially the negative ones and the thoughts of the past. Thoughts of the past will hold us hostage in our present state of being. You can be in a beautiful new home, working the job of your dreams, and all of a sudden become depressed because you start to believe you are what happened to you back then. The only time we should look back over our lives, is to see where we've come from. God is always doing a new thing in our lives, if we're willing to let our lives be interrupted. We must surrender our thoughts and agendas to His will. We have the creative ability to change course, switch directions, transform, and become something new. Allow your life to be interrupted in order to become a better version of you.

Often times, I listen to Pastor Steven Furtick, of Elevation Church in Charlotte, NC. His messages are based on the word of God, and his deliverance is one that is so motivating it moves crowds like the ones you see at an NFL football game. Pastor Furtick's messages have impacted my life in such a radical way that I'm compelled to share with others, who are eager to overcome anything in life with victory.

It was a typical day at work with the same annoying co-workers, intimidated by my light, who were inviting me to their normal "misery party." Misery loves company and I don't accept those invitations, but the heat was being turned up so much on the inside of me that I found myself feeling backed against the wall, and I wanted to come out swinging. I shook the thoughts and emotions trying to overcome me, so I wouldn't react the way they wanted me to. He who angers you, controls you, and I wasn't willing to give up my power to those who thought they had some. I tried to ignore the ignorance coming at me and switched my thoughts from "react to proact." I put my earbuds in and waited for Pastor Furtick's latest sermon to load with great anticipation. I believed God would have a message tailor-made for me to help me understand what was going on around me. I honestly remember hearing the words, "promotion and all of this is preparing me for something greater on the inside of me." When Pastor Furtick started preaching, he said something so profound that my spirit leaped. He said, "If you plow, he will promote you. It's the preparation that gets you ready for the promotion." God was using this season in my life to prepare me. The preparation doesn't always look like the promise, but I had to stay on my post and point my focus towards the plow. If you plow and look back, you're not fit for the kingdom. I didn't want that to be my story, so I plowed all the more. I didn't look back, or even think back to the things they wanted me to take personally. I just kept plowing as if I was working for God and not with them. They had no idea how I could move with such grace, style, and class after they constantly tried to provoke me. They wanted me to feel less valuable than I was because they weren't confident enough in their own abilities. Comparison is and will always be the thief of all joy. They had no idea I was letting His will be done on Earth as it was in Heaven. The natural mind cannot discern the things of the spiritual mind and I was thinking on the spiritual level. Greater is He that is within me than he that is in the world. I was doing what I had to do in this season. I had to humble myself when I didn't see the point, but I was persistent in the process no matter how relentless the oppressor was. They could not win against my God or the assignment placed on my life. Nothing I was going through was going to be wasted. God was working in my life and was preparing me to prevail. I had to aim my focus not on the problems, but on the victories and the one who gives victory. I had to stay with it because I trusted God and wanted him to trust me with more. Until I became faithful where I was, no matter how hostile the environment seemed, God would not promote me because I wasn't ready. If I reacted to everything that was done to me, instead of standing still in the presence of

God and allowing Him to fight my battles for me, God would not be able to trust me with more because I didn't know how to handle what I had now. God was cultivating me in those challenging moments, and if God is cultivating you right now—where you are—allow Him to. Your life is being interrupted.

Life Interrupted:
LOVE IS THE GREATEST

I WILL NEVER STOP believing in love no matter how many times I've experienced the opposite. We were created by love (God) and for love (God and his people). If I were to stop loving, my heart and this world would become cold, and there would be no reason for me to live. Love is what drives me. It is my passion and it comes with surrender, tranquility, peace, sacrifice, hurt, and joy. It conquers the forces of evil and hate, as love always prevails. Love lifted me. When nothing else could help, love lifted me. Self-love was the love I needed to get back to, in order to receive the kind of love I wanted. I had to love myself more, so that anything less than the kind of love I gave myself could not infiltrate my life as an imposter of love. I wanted the real deal. I was finally ready for real love.

The enemy of love is hate. Hate wants us to experience the opposite of love so much that we start believing it doesn't exist. It wants us to reciprocate hate in order to drive out the light of love. When you walk into a dark room it only takes one flick of the switch to transform that darkness into light. Love will never stop existing. Under the toughest exteriors, lie some of the most beautiful souls, desperate for love. Love covers, but also exposes. While we're still on this journey navigating through life, I often wonder if we numb our own pain, feelings, voices, and desires to help others, who we would not normally be in the position to love, back to life. We have to first love ourselves and recognize the emotions and desires on the inside of us, as either healthy or not healthy. Unhealthy emotions show up in our lives and can wreak havoc on ourselves and our relationships. We sabotage ourselves and others when we don't deal with our unhealthy emotions and allow them to take control of us. God gave us emotions to use in times of happiness, sadness, anger, love, and fear, but we are not to let our emotions use or rule us. I was guilty of being strong for everyone else, while neglecting my own weaknesses. I was guilty of not exposing my deepest, darkest secrets, for fear of judgement or lack of credibility. When it came to helping others, I wanted to be viewed as a shero: a strong, superwoman with love as her most powerful weapon. I didn't want to reveal my kryptonite to the village I was saving. I wanted them to think I had no weaknesses because my ego was fighting for my soul just as much as love was. I had to choose which one would win. I let my ego lose and love won.

I've learned to just accept people for who they are, not how they appear to be, or how we desire them to be. I had to allow people to accept me the same. With the good comes the bad, ugly, and indifferent. How beautiful this world would be, if we would take our own ideals and perceptions off of others, without reservations or judgements. People would freely be themselves, knowing you accept them in moments of vulnerability and strength. Ego teaches us that if we don't reach the status quo, then we are less than. We must unlearn some of the things we've absorbed, including what our parents taught us. Parents don't know everything, and oftentimes, they pass down wrong teachings from the generation before them and the cycle continues.

Love will lead you to truth, because the truth is love. Each of us has a deposit of love on the inside of us, and the spirit of truth is always guiding us, if we're open enough to receive it. Allow real love to interrupt your life.

9

Life Interrupted:
THE IMPORTANCE OF FORGIVENESS

Forgiveness is a friend to confidence. When you forgive yourself and others, you are able to confidently see yourself and others around you in a positive light. Since perceptions shape your reality, your reality becomes shaped by what you perceive to be true about yourself and others. The truth is, we will all make mistakes and a lesson will repeat itself until it's learned. While we are learning we will experience growing pains. The key is to grow from it, and not be ashamed of it.

Truthfully, I wanted a gallon of love, but most could only give me a cup. It wasn't that they didn't want to give me a full gallon, they just weren't able to because they didn't know how to. I forgave him, and I forgave myself, and by doing that our lives were interrupted. I started being okay with functioning through criticism. I was finally ready to live in my truth, have some courage, and let people know we were no longer together. I started embracing the unconventional me. Sometimes, we forget we're made in God's image. I was poised and didn't let anyone see me sweat. I was responding in calm ways and ruling my temperament. Forgiveness is a strength, not a weakness. I was unapologetic for my decisions. While everyone else was saying, "I'm sorry." I responded with, "I'm not." There was no love lost between us, only a relationship. I wasn't being called to patch a marriage and I could no longer say, "God, please fix it."

The God in me was being called to repair it, and repairing it meant being brave enough to leave it. Life interrupted means things aren't going to change, unless you change it first. While many call on a God outside of them to step down from heaven and save them, the real savior is within. You're waiting on God, while God is waiting on you. I had to overcome ME. My soul starting thirsting for God and God alone. What I wanted and what I was worth were two different things. I started subconsciously wanting things from a place of need. I knew deep down inside I was worth every vision and every dream I had of love. It was pictured in my head and I knew someone had it to offer.

I'm not perfect and I often fall short, but I handled my business and stood by someone's side, who was incapable of handling there's. I believed, in my heart of hearts, that I was hanging in there for love because he needed it more than I did. A part of me felt I needed to give him more love to help make up for the lack of love he'd received as a child. Another part of me felt his broken love was the best love he could give and the last part of me realized that I didn't like love in parts. My life was being interrupted with a love so powerful and needed that it couldn't be filled by any physical being. I surrendered in that moment and accepted the love of God and the healing power that came with it. I became the woman I knew I could be, the one who didn't need a man to feel complete. I was full of loving myself and ready for the right kind of love as I fell back in love with my "maker."

"Dear God, thank you for interrupting."

10

Rewrite
THE SCRIPT

Looking at the characters in my life, I started to do an assessment. I was in between two parallel worlds, feeling like I was in heaven while also walking the earth. I wasn't being double minded. I decided to let go of anyone who appeared to be selfish in my world and instead, chose to gravitate towards anyone who was selfless. Why go on with people who claim they love you, when their actions speak to the contrary? There were people in my life that were okay with being "normal" and didn't mind conforming to what this world teaches us to be. However, there was something about me that I knew was non-conforming. I never wanted to fit in, yet I found myself fitting in just enough to be liked and make others feel comfortable. As long as we were on the same level we wouldn't have any issues, but the moment

I wanted better for myself and began to grow, it became a problem for them. I wasn't sure if they didn't want me to grow and go, or if they just didn't want to be left behind. I realized I was the strongest and smartest person in the midst of all the people around me because I had the need to feel like I was leading others by making myself appear smaller. There was no one I associated with that I aspired to be like, there was no one in that group of people that could challenge me or lead me to my destiny. It was time to create healthy boundaries with the people in my life, no matter if it caused tension because I was coming into a place that was good for my soul.

Most people in my life have grown because of me. I've given them food for thought, but what did they give me? My growth came from the pain of helping others to the point of feeling insane. I was seeing people for their potential, instead of accepting them right where they were. The dangers in that was, what if they're comfortable with where they are and never intend on turning their potential into purpose? I vowed to always see the good in people, but also to never settle for someone's potential, again. It is important to be around people who are already doing the things I aspire to do, or are successful and can teach me something I didn't know. It was time to fly. I could no longer dim my light for others. It was time for them to put on their shades if I was shining too bright.

"Begin with the end in mind." It is a phrase my mother began saying to me at a very young age. Although, I didn't always apply this concept in my adult life, I oftentimes found myself circling back to her words of wisdom. Every journey that is successful begins with the end in mind. When you begin with the end in mind, you'll see that no matter what you go through in life, God will use it to reveal His glory. Stay on the road. You may not understand all the reasons, but stay on the road. Sometimes we miss God, because we look for Him in the dreams, but where He's found is in the disappointments. Don't allow your story to be over and don't judge the journey before it begins. You have to wait and see what the end will bring. If you trust His promises, then you have to trust His path. It might be winding, it might not feel good, and it might not be spectacular, but He's the God of details and detour that will lead to the cross you must bear. I "Keri" my cross. Sometimes you'll see it in the broken places and the scars, more than you'll see it in the blessed places. Your eyes will be opened and then you'll recognize Him and see that he's with you every mile in this journey.

11

Life Interrupted:
RELIGION VS. RELATIONSHIP

I'VE MET MANY people in life that have a religionship with God, instead of a relationship. They attend church services regularly, while praying to an eternal God they only believe exists in a building, such as a church. They think that if God felt like it, He would come down from heaven to save us. These individuals don't understand the true power of a living God. He is living inside of us and therefore Heaven does exist on Earth. They are oblivious to the fact that they have the same resurrecting power that God has. They have the ability to transform and change their circumstances, but they can't see it. They believe being religious out of tradition is enough in this life. I've seen some of the most miserable people try their best to act happy. I've seen some call on "Jesus" while still living the same defeated lives day in and day out. A relationship with God is one that works on a two-way street. It is reciprocal.

You pray, serve, love, walk, and talk with God. You silence all other voices and start listening for the voice of God. Not only do you listen for the voice, you look for it as well. God will speak in the most unconventional ways. I've heard him speak through strangers, billboards, and nature. God created us to worship Him, therefore we do. We worship Him in all that we say and do, as reflections of His beings. You're open and transparent with God because after all, you can't hide anything from the spirit of God, nor can you run from it. You also realize having a vertical relationship with God enhances your lateral relationships with other human beings. There is a calling on your life you don't get to shake. You were uniquely created as a fearful and wonderful human being by the Creator of this universe. We are all interconnected and a part of one another. Don't spend another moment playing by all the rules. Instead, spend your moments in tune with the gifts you were given that no one else in this world has but you. You were sent to accomplish this very thing by a Creator that knew you before you were formed in your mother's womb.

We were taught to go to school, graduate from college, and work for corporations while helping to build their success. At the end of the day, we feel unsatisfied after helping companies reach their business goals because we're unhappy with not reaching ours. We must allow ourselves to fully operate in our gifts that were deposited in us if we want to fully experience a life of love that comes with purpose. Get started by serving others and finish strong by knowing there will be roadblocks along the way that are designed to build your character, not break you. Get united with other like-minded individuals because there's strength in numbers when you don't have enough strength of your own. That's what a relationship with God will do for you. It will inspire you to make moves instead of waiting for moves to be made for you. Religion taught me to stay in my broken marriage: "For better or for worse." I continued to suffer and work while my spouse didn't. Many women continue to take care of the children, while allowing the man to become complacent because we tell ourselves that we should love a person from where they are, not where we want them to be. We continue to ignore that he's unstable financially and mentally. We look past the debt and legal issues he's brought into our home. Religion made me feel like I was stuck; There was no way out because I said, "I do" in a courthouse before God.

A relationship with God made me realize I was too valuable to not love myself enough to want better for myself. The Creator of this universe perfectly created me and wanted me to enjoy the love, life, and happiness that was deposited in me since the beginning of time. I felt like I was being pulled in two opposite directions. One arm was being tugged saying, "Stay in your mess," while the other arm was grabbed saying, "Follow me for peace." I was at a crossroads and desperately wanted to be rescued, but the only way that would happen was if I listened to my soul and followed the one that created it. The moment I said, "There has got to be something better than this," was the moment things started getting crazier.

It seemed like every year my spouse was arrested for something, but that particular year he was arrested the week I was moving out of the internal prison I was in and into my external new home. While he was away, I felt freedom and nervousness at the same time. When I settled in my new home, I thought to myself, had he not been in jail, I wouldn't have had the strength to leave because he would have followed. Out of that tragic situation my prayers were answered, the stars aligned, and I was able to move. I didn't just move physically, I moved mentally, emotionally, and spiritually. My life was interrupted, and I was awakened, not by what religion taught me, but by the relationship God had with me. God is a gentleman and forces himself on no one, which is why he gives us free will. We have to be willing to make a move, if we want God to move on our behalf.

12

Life Interrupted:
FROM PAST TO FUTURE

Look back, but only to remember how far you've come. The more I looked back at my situation, the harder it was to keep hope alive for my future. I would descend to my lowest self, instead of rising to the high calling of God in my life. There are times when I know I still need help because no man is an island, but I'm no longer trapped. The universe started revealing everything necessary for my anointing, my calling, my power, and direction through the spirit of God. I started to believe everything God said about me, regardless of my past mistakes and failures. I simply misunderstood my assignment by aligning myself with individuals I needed to flee from. True accountability happens when you are no longer blaming others for circumstances you helped to create. I was an enabler: I saw red flags and still went for it, only to wave the white flag of surrender before it was too late. I settled for less than what I desired because I didn't know how priceless and valuable I was. When I look back over my life, it's a wonder I made it out of some of the dire circumstances I was involved in. If I replayed them over and over again in my head, it could be downright depressing. Now, when I look back over my life, I look to see how far I've come, and I remind myself to never go back again. We are naturally creatures of habit, so there were things coming my way, trying to test my faith, to see if I had truly begun a new chapter in my life. I found myself in familiar circumstances that reminded me of who I used to be: a people pleaser. It was now time to please God because every time I pleased myself or someone else, God was not pleased. I learned some great lessons from my enemies and my life experiences. Every fragmented piece of my life was being used by God to take away the old and form something new, and although I didn't know what this new life would bring, I was certain my future was going to be better than my past.

An excerpt from "Soul"

The time we spent together was like the sun that nurtures a dying
plant as it grows new life into this Earth
I like a bird on a flight in search for that treetop to nest the new life into
this world or like a baby taking his and her first step as Mother and
Father watch with pride knowing that the Lord will send forth an angel
to guide them through the unknown that lies ahead
Loving you is like taking my last breath knowing that each kiss you get
gives no fresh air to my lungs and each touch will keep my heart beating
at a pace that only you can feel
With you my soul has found that even in my deepest sleep I'm never lost
you are my ying and yang Eternal
A 360 degree rotation that continues to spin around my universe giving
me the four seasons
An undying love that only one can feel if he or she really knows what
real love feels like and if forever this is real love then I am blessed to
have had an angel like you to keep me focused on tomorrow knowing
that today could be my last so I'll go
I'll go knowing that a love that was once filled with nothing was
replaced with everything that I missed on this journey to wherever it
was I was trying to get to for the moment but diverted by your sunshine
that opened my eyes to the fact that Angels do walk the earth and you
forever will be mine.

—Soul

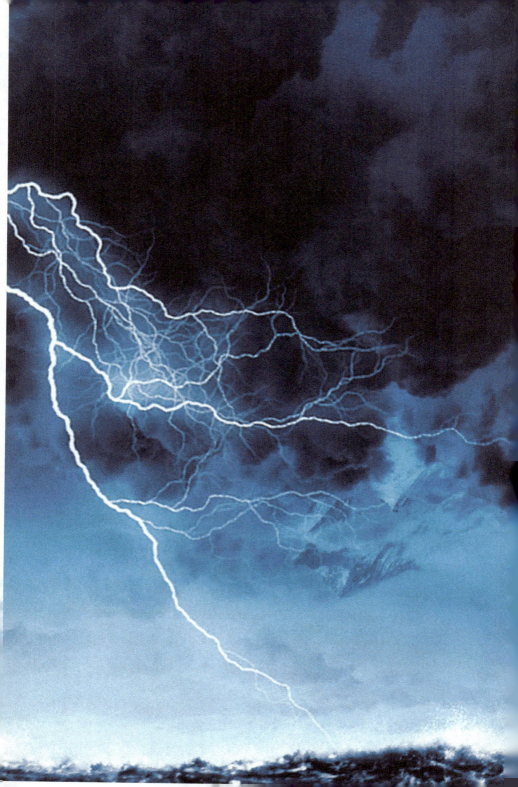

13

Life Interrupted:
FIRST TIME PARENTS

There are no blueprints or handbooks when you become a parent for the first time. When you bring a new life into this world and see your child for the first time it is the most amazing experience that one could ever have. Just as the flowers bloom, they grow with time, love, and care. You start to wonder if you're planting and tending your garden as you should in order to help it grow. You realize life is no longer about you and every decision you make impacts the little lives you've created so you lead by example. When you do, you'll notice your children tend to follow suit. Sometimes children do things parents didn't teach them at all, there's a little foolishness bound up in the heart of a child that tells them to "try it." After they do, there's also a consciousness that tells them if that was right or wrong. As parents, we must realize that these treasures God gave us ultimately still belong to Him as the creator. Because of that we have to allow our children to do some things on their own.

A parent's job is to give their children the resources and tools they'll need as foundations, but we must realize our children's minds, hearts, and souls are their own. Children will make decisions that will have nothing to do with what their parents taught them. The best thing parents can do is allow them to learn the lesson in order for their child to get back up again. It's scary to sit back and try to view the world through a child's eyes, when parents believe they know better. It's also refreshing to see things from children's untainted perspectives. We have to trust that God still has a plan for our children's lives, even when it seems like our lives are being interrupted by their illogical decisions. Dedicate your children's lives to God. After all, He entrusted them to you, so why not trust them in His hands? One of my favorite pastimes with my children is watching movies together and looking at the excitement, emotion, and joy in their eyes. The feeling of experiencing a new world through their eyes brings playfulness back to our souls. Children allow us to experience unconditional love like never before, and no matter how upset you make each other, the relationship between parent and child is irreplaceable. While we thought we chose to become parents, our children actually chose us since there is a separation between body and spirit. They were with God in the beginning, a place where there is no time. Then, He released them unto parents at the proper time. Ready or not, here they come! We have a great responsibility to raise productive members of society that could leave legacies for the next generation to come. Once life is interrupted with newborn seeds, parents will never be the same again as this is an extended branch of your family tree.

14

Life Interrupted:
THE SINGLE PARENT SYNDROME

It was intended for mothers and fathers to procreate and raise children together, but there's a startling statistic of how many mothers and fathers are doing this alone. I became a part of that statistic during my marriage and afterwards. While I was still married, I felt like a single parent taking the load of the responsibilities for our children. My husband had no car, license, or job and was okay with me doing everything for them. After my life was interrupted and I moved into my new home, I was still a single parent; the only difference was there wasn't a man in the home. I thought to myself, "How many women are holding down the fort with a man in the home that doesn't contribute to the household? How did we get to a place where we feel it's okay to take care of everyone except ourselves? Who taught us that?

Why did we believe this lie?" There are many women that believe it's better to have a male around, even if he hasn't fully developed into a man, instead of doing it all by themselves. I had to be shaken in order to be shifted from that mentality. As much as I didn't want to become a single parent, I was willing to become one for the sake of my peace of mind and for my daughters to not repeat my mistakes. I wanted better for them, and more importantly, I wanted better for me. My life was interrupted and when I decided to do what was best for me, it also became the best for everyone around me.

My children couldn't understand what was happening at first. We continued counseling, so they could express what they were really feeling. I tried my best to keep them busy and their minds focused on other things besides the separation. Despite my efforts, my youngest daughter's behavior was getting worse, and my oldest seemed to have an attitude that she hadn't displayed before. I knew the road to recovery was going to be a long one and it wasn't going to be easy; however, I also knew I couldn't go back to what we once knew. I explained to my daughters this was now our new normal and although Mommy and Daddy weren't together anymore, we still loved them. Their dad is still a part of their family and I'm doing the best I can to make sure we're both there for them.

At times, one of the parents may feel they want to make the separation about themselves. There were numerous calls and texts sent to me that weren't about our children, but more about how much he still loved me, how he was sorry, and how he wanted me to take him back. Other texts were more hostile with him lashing out at me, stating that I never loved him in the first place. He would go on about his new employment and how he could now give me money I'd so desperately asked for before our separation. Some days I would respond to the text with a simple, "Please check on your kids, not me," and other days I wouldn't respond at all.

Our kids would call and ask their dad to come and get them. Some days he would stand them up and other days he came up with an excuse as to why he couldn't pick them up. I told myself not to speak negatively about him to our children, but I would no longer make excuses for him either. It wasn't my job to preserve his reputation with them. They had to see the disappointment for themselves, so they could fully understand why Mommy had to remove herself from that equation. I'm sure he had the best intentions to see his children, even when it felt like minimal effort to me. They, however, didn't care about the excuses. All they saw was the bottom line and that was daddy didn't come today like he said he would. I tried to overcompensate for his lack of involvement, only to realize I could never take his place. Nothing would ever compare to the love daughters have for their fathers. They didn't care about how much money he had; all they wanted was the first man they had ever loved. My feelings for my father were the same. No matter what he did or how often he let me down, I would never give up on him or stop loving him. Whenever he did come around, all was forgiven. It was as if he had been there the entire time, and that was all that mattered.

Society has taught us that the outcome of single parent homes can lead to some children having behavioral issues that later turn into adult issues. That does not mean that every two-parent home has perfect children that don't have behavioral issues. The low economic status that some are subjected to, such as public housing due to a single parent's income, oftentimes leads to poverty, higher crime rates, and violence. Education is compromised when they're forced to attend failing schools based on the school districts they live in. Some single parents learn to be so independent, doing it all on their own— myself included—that we're not open enough to receive the help we need. Pride sets in and before long a fall comes. On the other hand, because single parents are raising children alone, some feel entitled to receive handouts. The "somebody owes me something" mentality has given people permission to receive assistance without ever having to make a plan to assist themselves. It is a system that is easily manipulated, and it works by excusing them from having to become more of who they were destined to be. Complacency sets in and comfort feels cozy. They feel abandoned by the one who procreated with them and become ignorant and blinded by bitterness, while gravitating towards easy living. That pull towards the easy road is so strong that they're willing to forfeit their purpose by not showing up ready to believe it's possible to come out of this situation better than they started. Somebody, somewhere in the world needs them.

Life interrupted begins when you're no longer looking for handouts, but instead you have your hand out! Your hand is out to serve, to lead, to receive resources that will help educate and elevate you above your normal circumstances. Life interrupted allows us to be open enough to receive love again after having the wrong kind of love leave us. Someone walking out on us, making us single parents, leaves many burdens to bear, but that does not mean that's the end of the story. It means we get to rewrite our stories by learning from the experience and empowering someone else along the way that may find themselves in a similar situation. If you want your new story to be a true love story, you must forgive your past, assume the best about the person who offended you, and move on. Your children deserve that and so does the world you serve. Once you're in this place, you're ready to receive the kind of love that you may have taken for granted if the wrong kind of love didn't leave. Allow what you thought was love to walk out of your life in order for true love to walk in, allow real love to interrupt your life and you will appreciate it all the more.

15

Life Interrupted:
ONCE WAS LOST, BUT NOW FREE

YOU HEAR THE sirens and see the blue lights. Your heart is racing fast and your stomach drops. You hear the words, "You're under arrest and have the right to remain silent." Do you feel fear? Do you shed a tear? Do you feel like the end is near? You're handcuffed, booked, and put into a cell. Life as you knew it became interrupted and will never be the same. You're now between bars when just moments ago you felt wind from the outside air, saw people standing in front of their houses, and cars parked in the driveway. Then, it starts to settle in that the grass ain't always greener on the other side. As a matter of fact, there is no grass on the other side. You're now in an institution where nothing around you seems to be growing. It's a place designed to rehabilitate, but feels like a place that decapitates. It tears people into bits and pieces: stripping them of their mind and dignity, while questioning their character and integrity, and disrespecting their bodies by humiliating their souls. Things start to feel out of control.

My experience with those that have been to prison has been enlightening. While many in today's society turn their backs on this population, I seek to understand the criminal, or in some instances, not so criminal mind. I have relatives sentenced to life in prison, and when we communicate through letters their minds appear to be free. When freedom is taken away, the things inmates used to take for granted, such as their intelligence, now becomes something they think about often. They reminisce on the life they had and the life that's ahead. They now have a choice for their minds to take them higher or lower, and it all depends on how they view their circumstances: perspective is key. On the one hand, an inmate is likely to get out of jail and go back to a life of crime because their chance of surviving in the free world is surrounded by a stigma. A convicted felon now has to check a box on a job application that states they are in fact someone who committed a past crime. Despite the fact that they paid their debt to society, they still have to wear the label. This type of branding lessens their likelihood of getting a decent paying job and becoming a productive member of society. The act of checking that box damages their mental state as well as they start to believe that their past mistakes are who they are. Society labels them and thus they label themselves. Not long afterwards, they begin to lose confidence in their ability to become law abiding citizens and go into survival of the fittest mode because it's almost impossible for them to make a decent living and be treated as first class citizens. These human beings become dehumanized and will do anything to feed themselves, their families, and to feel valued again. This tends to lead back to a life of crime and the cycle continues.

Life interrupted begins for an inmate who realizes his mind and soul are free no matter how long the jail sentence or the lack of freedom they feel when released. He or she knows that their problems are no match for God and the life of controlled environments does not compare to the life to come. They realize there is a life after this and there is a life they can have right now, even while behind bars. There are some highly intelligent prisoners I've met along the way, who understood the gift of time and how they should use it while locked up. I've noticed I don't always discipline my free mind to focus on purpose and destiny due to many distractions in the world. Some prisoners use the gift of time to discipline every area of their life. They also realize just because they're locked up doesn't mean their talents are wasted; there are people inside of the prison walls that still need their gifts. The rehabilitated inmate isn't someone that serves their time and then commits the same crimes again. The rehabilitated inmate is someone who is transformed from the inside out, who realizes that although life was interrupted and has taken a turn, that turn can be used for good. Their life has been interrupted to show them that the same time and energy they put into the wrong things can be used for the right things, and to help release someone else along the way.

16

Life Interrupted:
A RELATIONSHIP WITH MONEY

I NEEDED A BETTER relationship with money, so I had to start viewing it differently than I did in my past. My former relationship was one that didn't consist of budgeting, saving, or giving. I thought money was just a means to buy things and pay bills, yet I was missing out on the most important aspect of money, which was to invest in things and get a return on my investment. As frugal as I thought I was, I realized if I held too tightly to the money I had, I wouldn't have the room to receive more money because my fists were too tightly closed. I was too afraid of losing what I already had because I was the only person taking care of myself and my daughters. Without a second income, my money was being used and abused and that always left me living paycheck to paycheck without any savings in case of emergency. The law of reaping and sowing only applies when we first sow, so we can reap the benefits of the seed that was given. My life was interrupted by changing my thought process towards giving. I began tithing at churches, giving to charities, and dedicating my time and resources to people and things in need. Those were fertile seeds in good soil that were starting to produce a harvest in my life that brought me so much joy! I saw money as something that was not supposed to sit and stay still, instead it was supposed to flow from one source to another and multiply. I began to stop spending foolishly on things I wanted and instead started spending money on things I needed and applied any extra income to my outstanding debt. I still don't like to pay full price for anything! I didn't want to become a slave to money and that is what debt is. You are indebted to your debtors and can't live the abundant life that you desire to have when you have a cloud of debt hovering over you limiting your abilities and resources. It's very unfortunate that most of us weren't taught early on to value, invest, give, and save money the way that we should have, but once your life is interrupted with, "I'm sick of being broke and living check to check," you start to make the necessary changes in order to shift your perspective and change the outcome of your financial situation. My desire was to move from "just enough" to "more than enough." I want to leave an inheritance for generations to come and when I depart this Earth, I want the things I invested in to stand and be a testament to the kind of life I lived.

There are still many things I need to learn when it comes to taking risks, investing, and residual income, but the key thing is to take the first step towards having a better relationship with money. Once you do, more wisdom and knowledge are gained, and you can apply what you've learned about money and have it grow and flow in and out of your life. When money starts growing and flowing, you'll be in a better position to live the type of life you desire for yourself and others. It's a wonderful feeling knowing you've enhanced someone else's life along the way because you can now afford to give to them. The return is priceless, as this person is now in a better position than they were before and can pay it forward. That's what allows your investment to come back full circle and multiply, which in turn makes the world a better place.

17

Life Interrupted:
CONNECTING WITH SOULS

I'VE HAD THE very fortunate experience of traveling to different countries on mission trips, in the hopes of transforming and enhancing the quality of someone else's life. Nothing brings me more pleasure than knowing I've helped my fellow man along the way. I have a servant's heart, and giving my time, talent, and resources are something that I'm passionate about. Giving, serving, and loving on others is a gift from God, and when used as often as possible it makes our lives fuller. My experiences around the world have opened my eyes and allowed me to embrace diversity and culture as learning tools. Learning from those who are different from me has broadened my perspective, as well as increased my tolerance and acceptance, which has allowed me many teachable moments. We may have different skin colors, personalities, and beliefs, but what keeps us connected is our ability to freely open up our minds, hearts, and souls so that we may receive something different from our brothers and sisters all over the world. While the ego divides, the spirit unifies us in the direction of love, and love is the most powerful thing on this earth.

It is every human being's responsibility to help someone else in need. We are meant to connect with those who we can help and those that can help us. Some will be in your life briefly, while others may last through eternity, but regardless of the time you spend together, there will be some souls you come across that will create permanent imprints on your heart, even if you never see them again; those are the divine connections we should all be looking for. My life was interrupted by this concept because I realized I didn't fit in where I was from or where I had been. I had to keep moving forward to wherever my dreams would take me. There are many people that refuse to come off their porch for fear of flying. Well, I do not fear flying; I want to fly and if it doesn't go well then, it's just another lesson learned, which helps to propel me into the next place I'm heading. Never settle or get comfortable with the current relationships you have; be open to receive that stranger that comes along, for they may be able to teach you more in just one encounter than those you've surrounded yourself with and been listening to your entire life. I know a part of my purpose is to travel the world and spread light and love, while giving to those less fortunate than myself. The reward is to reap the same, as I connect with souls much different than myself. It's a beautiful life to live and I'm forever grateful for it.

18

Life Interrupted:
CAREER VS. PURPOSE

SOCIETY TEACHES US to do well in school, go to college, get a good job, buy a nice home, drive a nice car, and have a family. The picture that society paints of what success looks like is quite different than the kind of success our Creator desires us to have. While many are ambitiously seeking titles, power, and money to make themselves look good on the outside, they're dying on the inside as their purpose lays dormant and their gifts go unused. We get stuck in an endless cycle of trying to keep up with the Joneses, unable to realize that money and possessions won't buy happiness, even though that's the formula the world teaches us. There are many people with well-paying jobs, who you would assume are living the high life, but the trick to success is actually enjoying the money that comes with it. Most fail at enjoying life because the stress and the need to make more, do more, and be more is an ever-present struggle. Godliness with contentment equals great gain. Society teaches us that the more we acquire, the happier we'll become, but it's all an illusion. The true key to happiness is to discover the very thing that was deposited in you since the beginning of your time and to utilize that while you're on Earth. There is something very unique about each and every one of us that only we have and only we can do to serve the world. Once you discover that gift, it begins to make room for you. There are people in this world that are in need of the gift you have to offer, which is a part of your purpose. When you live a life of purpose, every decision you make is intentional. You're able to minimize distractions and block out the many voices that are trying to tell you who you are and who you should be. You stop looking for validation from others: friends, career, television, radio, and any other outside opinion. You have a confidence about yourself that comes from the solid foundation of knowing who you are and what you were created to do. There is no need to keep up with the Joneses or try to compete with others. You stay in your own lane because you know that in your lane you're strongest, most needed, most wanted, and most resourceful. If God intended us to be like everyone else the world, it would be a pretty boring place, so stop trying to keep up with celebrities, the wealthy, reality tv, or anything other than what you were called to do in this world. There is an overabundance of depressed rich people in the world. However, there's a difference between being rich and being wealthy. The rich have money, while the wealthy have an abundance of joy, peace, love, and happiness that doesn't revolve or depend on money or material assets. Instead of living the full lives they are capable of living, the rich believe that what they have is what makes them who they are. Things do not make us; character, integrity, morals, and values are what makes us. It's time to step out of the twilight zone and realize you were perfectly created by a perfect Creator, and since He can't make anything bad, how dare we think bad about ourselves because we aren't living up to society's expectations? We have to live up to our own and that comes from a voice on the inside of you that will guide you every step of the way as long as you're willing to listen. The Holy spirit will not call you to go deeper if you're not ready. Allow your life to be interrupted by opening up your mind, heart, and soul to the very One who created you so that you may live with purpose.

When you find yourself unmotivated and dispassionate about the job you do every day, you begin to feel exhausted and unfulfilled: a slave to the mundane routine. There are times you may feel stress or tension on the job because you're trying to remain comfortable in a place God wants you to leave. He makes you uncomfortable in order to get you to move. When that shift begins to occur, your life is being interrupted and beg you to allow it. The results are amazing. I am proud to say that I took a leap of faith and risked the stability of a paycheck every week from my nine to five job in order to pursue my dream and I am happy to say that many of my friends have taken that leap as well; I admire them for it. It was not an easy decision or undertaking. Some of us had to come up with action plans, budgets, and discipline in order to make the businesses run successful. I had to leave a job where I was an expert in my field and start fresh at a new place in a new area that I didn't know much about.

Originally, I was in a place where others were being brought in making more money than me, but they were less qualified. I had to train new people who received higher positions and better pay than I did. These people tried to sabotage my career by attempting to change things that weren't broken. I had to humble myself and know that things were falling apart so they could actually come together. This was working for my good, even if I couldn't see it at the time. The reason some of my new co-workers were being hateful, disrespectful, and demeaning towards me was because of the light I shared each day. It was intimidating for them to see others love me. They wanted an environment that was divided, but what I had created was welcoming. They were in it for position and power, but I was in it for purpose and provision, and not just provision for myself, but provision and guidance for the employees that needed it most. I felt my job wasn't complete unless I inspired, empowered, and connected with someone along the way. If their lives weren't better because of something I said or did, what was the point? My team, which didn't feel like a team at all, tried to keep in me in a box that I knew I had to break out of. I began to apply for positions in my field that I knew I didn't have the experience for or the specific qualifications, but the universe was calling me higher. God doesn't call the qualified; He qualifies the called. The next thing I knew, I was getting phone calls left and right for leadership roles such as Director of Workforce Development and other managerial positions. God's favor was upon me and he didn't want me to settle for mediocrity. He didn't want me to move on to another job with the same mindset that was holding me back. He wanted to elevate me because I carried myself with grace and elegance in the midst of hostile situations at my previous job. God could trust me to handle myself in a higher position because I focused on what was coming instead of what was happening. He was taking me to new levels, which required a new version of myself. I chose not to focus on the ones that tried to oppress me, instead I focused on the one that wanted to advance me.

The secret ingredient to taking a leap is faith. Faith to stop fearing and to start obeying what your gut is telling you to do. Faith to fail forward. If one idea or action doesn't work, you have to have enough faith to learn from that mistake and move forward by trying something different. You need enough faith to believe that no matter the return on your investment, if any, you are still going after what you believe your best life should be. At the end of the day, thank your haters, and let them be your motivators.

When I arrived at my new job, my purpose filled journey was put into action when one of my employees encountered abuse and came to work in despair. My title as Human Resources Manager didn't mean as much as the compassion, empathy, and sympathy I needed to show her. This was a pivotal moment in my career and in honor of the exchange we made through that conversation, I wrote her a letter. This letter not only represents her story, but countless others who feel trapped in a toxic relationship.

Dear R.W.,

THE DAY I spoke to you after hearing you were involved in a domestic violence situation was one of the most meaningful conversations I've ever had in my career. While the company wanted me to handle this situation before it crossed over into the workplace, I wanted to handle it because I knew this was something God required of me. It was deeper than work politics. It was about me coming out of a similar situation and being able to use my testimony to ignite a fire in you. I took a deep breath as I heard the pain and agony in your voice. I could relate to what you were going through and wanted you to know that I cared. You weren't alone, and your situation weighed heavily on my mind. You came to see me the next week and opened up to me in ways I didn't expect. I literally saw myself in you: someone trying to overcome a past that would continue to chase them until they gave in. But this time was different for you and I applaud your courage in getting a restraining order. At first, you didn't quit your job, but instead switched shifts to avoid interacting with your abuser. You were fragile, yet strong and brave. From my heart to yours, we shared stories. We were connected in that moment and each tear that fell released the old and opened our souls to the new. That shift confirmed your life was getting ready to change and I knew how critical every decision you made was. You would either move back into bondage or towards your freedom. You were taking the necessary steps that you could in order to protect yourself and that is not always easy, especially when you are trying to protect and love someone. I told you that the same love and loyalty you gave to that person, who didn't deserve it, you must now give to yourself. You must affirm yourself daily by replacing the negative images he tried to embed in you with positive ones. You must realize you are more than your circumstances, and you do not have to remain a victim. You were created as a beautiful human being to serve the world. Let the interruption of what was killing you, bring new life to you. You're on the road to healing. Healing is absolutely necessary, so be patient and gentle with yourself. Find those who genuinely love and support you as your spirit is renewed. Once you become the R.W. you were created to be, use the darkness you overcame as a powerful testimony to bring light to someone else. I love you. I'm proud of you, and I thank you for allowing me to serve you.

I recently contacted R.W. to see how she was doing because the road to recovery isn't always a clear, straight path. It is a road full of highs, lows, roadblocks, detours, and distractions. Her response was, "There are many days when I cry myself to sleep and don't recognize myself in the mirror. I lost a lot, including material things that were tied to him, but I know it was confirmation from God that it was time to start over. I can honestly say that I still struggle, while trying to overcome, yet I know I'm in a much better and happier place by myself than I ever was with him."

I want each reader to know they are not alone and there will be days you are challenged and struggle with the transformation process. However, there is light at the end of the tunnel and each day gets better as you move towards the life that was destined for you. Interrupt your life by ridding yourself of the old habits, thoughts, and people that tried to break you. The fact that you're still here is a testimony to the world that you have purpose far beyond your past circumstances.

19

Life Interrupted:
BEAUTY FOR ASHES

When you start to recognize the beauty of your soul, you start to recognize the beautiful souls around you. I remember when God interrupted my life. I was desperate to see things differently than the way I had before. In my case, I was heartbroken from a bad relationship in college and was starting to feel numb. I said, "God, if you're real, please come and save me." I was in my shower crying for so long that the water became cold and I didn't even feel it. After I got out of the shower, I called my mom to tell her how devastated I was because my college sweetheart and I had broken up. She apologized for the way I was feeling and advised me to go to church. I didn't grow up in the church and never took that part of the world seriously. I thought it was something people did out of tradition or because they were forced to go. However, the moment I asked God to come into my life something changed in my mind that made me believe God was real. Things around me began to look differently to me and so did the human race. No matter if people were good, bad, or indifferent towards me, I really sought to see the beauty in everyone. No matter how complicated this human race may seem there is something uniquely beautiful in each and every one of us. Had I not allowed God to interrupt my regularly scheduled program I might have turned to some other source of relief; it could have been drugs, alcohol, people, or food. I may have ended up depressed and in a dark place had I not allowed the light to enter. Our Creator made no mistake about the day we were born and the lives He intended for us to have. Regardless of who our parents are, or what backgrounds we've come from, we came into this world as blank canvases and some of us, unfortunately, learned some ugly things. Those things, however, are far from what really matters because our time on this Earth is temporary and they can be unlearned, as long as we're willing to seek the things that matter and leave the illusions behind. What do I mean by illusions, you ask? Greed, ulterior motives, selfish ambition, jealousy, envy, corruption, vanity, war, and many other prideful things are all rooted in darkness and have no real lasting effects. There is no light in any of that. "For what shall it profit a man, if he shall gain the whole world, and lose his own soul?" (Mark 8:36 KJV)

Life interrupted teaches us to get back to the light that created us; to reconnect with our heavenly family through spirit and in truth. The way to do that is to follow the spirit, even on cloudy days. The beautiful thing about the Holy Spirit is it's always waiting on us. When we search for it, we will find it; when we go deeper than the surface level, we'll find ourselves lifted to a higher consciousness. Once that happens, a shift occurs that changes the course of our lives forever. That's a powerful thing! To gain wisdom and knowledge from Heaven, as it was intended for all of God's creations, instead of striving to learn from the foolish things of this world. Life suddenly seems full of peace and unspeakable joy. Miracles occur once a person realizes they have a direct connection to God, especially when they once thought they were disconnected. Magic begins to happen when we align our hearts and minds with the Heaven we came from. The world becomes a better place when we allow God's healing to take place on the inside of us. When we know that God loves us beyond measure, we begin to love ourselves and spread that love to other people. When we're forgiven for the mistakes we've made, we extend that same grace and begin to forgive others. Life interrupted has the very intentional purpose of interrupting your life, so you can disrupt others in a mighty, powerful, and loving way.

An Excerpt
FROM "SOUL" IMPERFECTIONS

The Sun never shined bright on me like this before
They say there's no such thing as a perfect person
But I'll look in your eyes and all I see is perfection
I see the perfect world in your eyes
the perfect words that come from your lips with the perfect smile
The perfect movement with the perfect walk
the perfect tear that runs down your perfect skin
the way we hold each other at night and make love to the movement of
soft music to me it's nothing less than perfect
as weak as my heart is I never thought that I could ever love again
But you changed that and it's perfect
the bond between man and woman can only be described through my
eyes as perfect
now I understand there is no such thing as a perfect person
but I think you're a perfect person for loving and understanding this
imperfect person perfectly.

—Soul

20

Life Interrupted:
SOME TABLES DON'T TURN

It was Father's Day weekend and I was elated that my kids' father volunteered to keep our daughters for the rest of the summer. Not only would this give me a much-needed break, it would help me focus on the new job I was starting without having to balance motherhood. I was flying back from California when all of a sudden, feelings of sadness overcame me. When my uber driver dropped me off at my driveway, I walked into a big empty house. It wasn't filled with busyness, little feet running up and down the stairs, laughter and chaos as usual. It was eerily quiet. I was missing my children and my responsibilities as a mother. The very thing I was frustrated about, was the very thing I longed for: my children. I resisted the temptation of calling their father for as long as I could. I didn't want him to think

I didn't trust him with the kids on his own, nor did I want to interrupt their time together, since they weren't together often. I turned on the TV, did some laundry, and fixed something to eat, but I still couldn't shake the feeling of loneliness. Strange thoughts started to invade my mind. "You should just get back with your ex. The family doesn't have to be separated. It's better to be with someone than to be alone." Where did that come from? Before I could figure it out, my mind shifted to thoughts of my deceased brother. I began to wonder what he would be saying to me right now before starting my new job. That train of thought led me to realize that he no longer had to struggle with thoughts that would try to hold him hostage. The more my mind wandered, the sadder I became. The fact that it was Father's Day only made it worse, because I couldn't call my brother and wish him a happy one. He wasn't there to say, "let me speak to my nieces." My mind was racing, and I was overwhelmed with emotion. I started to pray, but felt no peace. I started to cry, but there was no release. I didn't know what to do, but I knew I couldn't continue to wrestle with thoughts that were not conducive to my well-being. I texted my ex to have our daughters call me. After hearing their voices and telling them I missed them, I asked to speak to their dad. I asked him to pray for me. I didn't want to call my parents and overwhelm them with the grief I was feeling about the loss of their son. I didn't want to call any friends either. I wanted to talk to my ex-husband to try and break the tension between us by asking him for a prayer. My hope was that maybe this would open the door for future communication. Oftentimes, my brother tried to be the mediator between my estranged husband and I, even though he didn't care for the man. So, I put my pride aside, cried, and allowed him to pray for me. He gladly accepted the invitation and said he missed my brother just as much as I did and could only imagine what I was going through. I didn't believe he missed my brother because they didn't have that type of relationship, but I did believe this was his attempt to be more empathetic towards me. He was the last person I thought I would reach out to in that particular moment, but for some reason my life was being interrupted with my thoughts and replaced with higher one's.

 Anytime you're willing to reinvent yourself and become a better person, it requires a new level of consciousness. It also requires humbleness by being the bigger person and releasing offenses to the power of God. God can use anybody, at any given moment, even if you thought that person was the enemy.

I felt a little relief after my ex prayed, and I hoped there would be a breakthrough. If he and I could reconcile, not as husband and wife, but as co-parents and friends it would be better and easier for our girls. Yet, things still felt awkward between us because he had a resistance about him that was obvious. It was apparent he was still angry and bitter towards me because I left an unhealthy marriage, he thought I should've stayed in. He didn't want to be accountable for his actions, nor the consequences of them. As he continued to play the blame game and refused to acknowledge his shortcomings, the womanizer cycle continued, but with someone else. I'm no longer concerned about what he's doing or who he's doing it with; I'm only concerned about our children. Whenever I attempted to have a conversation about our children, he would become uncooperative and hostile towards me. The emotional baggage he continued to carry from his past to different relationships did not solve his issues. Instead, he believed the new person to be the problem while ignoring the same behaviors and patterns that resurface in his life.

My brother's absence continued to remind me to take the high road. I have never asked my estranged husband for money or to do anything for our kids. God has always made a way through hard work, the support of my parents, and the village it takes to raise a child. The moment my ex used manipulation to try and make me look like a bad person to our children, I took the high road and allowed them to stay with him for the summer. By law I should have had a legal address showing me where they were living, but he wouldn't give me one. The fact that he wouldn't give me an address and told our girls not to tell me either, proved he was still in the same mental space he was in when I first met him. Because I was growing outside of our relationship, I assumed that by letting him go, he would grow as well, but he didn't. My growth and the separation only made him resentful. When I asked him to get our daughters' hair done before school started, because it would be one less thing for me to do, he had the audacity to tell me to "let go" and then hung up on me. I honestly laughed and thought to myself, "If he's moved on, then why is he so angry and difficult?"

The day before my deceased brother's birthday, he texted me inappropriate things and threatened to block my number from calling him. I assured him that I would take this information to the courts and reminded him about my legal rights as a parent. My concern was never about another woman, because I had emotionally checked out of our marriage five years prior to physically relocating. I couldn't have cared less about his relationship status and honestly, I pitied his latest victim. My concern was for him as a father wanting our children to keep a secret from me when I had every right to make sure they were in safe living conditions. That night, I asked God to forgive me for engaging in a conversation with a person that was not willing to change or think rationally. The conversation was counterproductive because misery loves company and I shouldn't have accepted the invitation. I released him to God and vowed to never behave like that again. As much as I wanted us to be mature enough to handle our affairs outside of court, I realized it was impossible with a person like him; the best thing for me to do was to let the courts decide how we dealt with one another. I woke up the morning of what would have been my brother's thirty-fifth birthday with extreme happiness and gratitude to celebrate his life instead of mourning his death. My estranged husband called and text me as if he hadn't behaved erratically the day before. He noticed the happy birthday posts on social media and reached out to me, pretending to care about my well-being. This was his typical bipolar, narcissistic, manipulative behavior. I ignored the messages and phone calls and stuck to my promise of not engaging with him again.

When dealing with difficult people and complex situations, you must realize that you can't change people, but you can change yourself, which in turn can change the outcome of your situation. Acceptance is key when life is interrupted. When you come to accept people and circumstances for the way they are, you must also accept that it does not give them permission to treat you as they always have. It gives you permission to say, "I accept this person for who they are, but I value myself enough to not be treated this way. I will accept this table not turning, but I will turn and walk away."

21

Life Interrupted:
WHEN YOU LET GO, THEY DON'T

A week and a half before school started, my youngest daughter said she didn't want to come back home; all of a sudden wanted to live with her dad. I asked why? She told me that Nalani, her older sister, didn't want her to. I told her they were just suffering from sibling rivalry and to not let her sister make her feel like she wasn't welcome home. They were just annoying one another, and it would eventually pass. She proceeded to tell me, "Daddy said I can stay, and he'll enroll me in gymnastics."

I thought to myself, "Yeah, right!" I knew the brainwashing would start at some point, but I also thought my daughters were smart enough to know better. I asked to speak to their father, but all he sent me was a text about enrolling her in school. Surely a conversation was needed and not text messages. I asked him to call me, and he said he couldn't at that moment. I assumed he was around the female he was trying to keep a secret, but that didn't bother me. What bothered me was that he didn't have a leg to stand on and wanted to get a reaction out of me concerning our daughter. When he finally called back, I gave him my concerns. I was worried about him being unstable and not having a place of his own. The moment the woman they were staying with decided she wanted her space, he and my children would be out on the street. Furthermore, he still wouldn't give me an address for where they were living, nor did he have enough respect to introduce me to the woman my children had been staying with for the past six weeks. What parent in their right mind would leave their child in another state without knowing where they lived? He didn't have any health insurance, life insurance, or steady income. It wasn't in his character to assist with homework or extracurricular activities. He also lacked the ability to exercise patience when it came to their needs and wants. However, I was still willing to revisit the subject in the future, if he was willing to do what was needed to make sure the girls were being provided for. Now, however, was not the right time.

He, of course, took my concerns and started to accuse me of being manipulative and spiteful. He claimed my behavior was the reason behind the lack of address and information as to where they were living. He actually had the nerve to say that he didn't have to give the children back to me. "Huh? What do you mean?" He had to be talking to himself and not me. There wasn't a manipulative or spiteful bone in my body. As for him not returning the children, school started in two weeks and the agreement was for him to keep them for the summer and not a minute longer. He knew that; he'd agreed to that.

"I'll fight for them," were the last words he said before he hung up the phone. I was devastated and didn't know what to do. Since we weren't legally divorced, there wasn't a court ordered custody agreement in place; so, technically, he had the same parental rights as I did. I cried, contacted lawyers for consultations, and realized I had to get divorced quickly. Whatever it took, I had to fast forward the process. A few days later he sent some manipulative message about not being my enemy. I responded with, "You sure are acting like one." I knew I couldn't give him any more of my energy. I gave it to the law instead. I will move Heaven and Earth for my children and that's exactly what I did. I prayed for three days and didn't sleep. By the time I spoke to my daughters again, my baby girl was ready to come home. God had answered my prayers.

Let this be a lesson learned to anyone going through a separation or divorce with children involved. When the other party shows you that they are not mature enough to co-parent, seek legal advice. Don't lose your cool when you can let the courts decide. Many of us don't want to go this route, but we also don't want our children to become casualties of war because it only hurts them in the long run. I never thought parenting would boil down to a court document telling us when and where we could have our children. However, it was necessary. I tried to give him the benefit of the doubt, but my kindness was taken for weakness and my kids were being used against me. He had nothing else on me to break me down, although he tried to break me during our entire marriage. He wanted to dim my light because he didn't have enough of his own to shine. I'm sure his version of love made him feel inferior to the superior things I was accomplishing, which is why he could never live up to what real love should be. It was all he could give.

Ladies and gentlemen, please work on yourselves, and be confident in who you are before going into someone else's world. When you do, you'll make their world better and yours becomes better in the process. If you don't work on your inner issues before joining someone else's world, you'll begin to envy the person you're supposed to love. You'll love from a place of dependency rather than authenticity. You'll begin to feel like a victim and start sabotaging your relationship because you will fear losing that person, since you believe they are better than you. When you make mistakes, you will expect them to pick up the broken pieces, but the problem is you never intended on fixing your brokenness. That has to come from within.

No matter how much I tried to inspire him, he continued to behave the way he did to hold me down. He wanted me to stay down with him, but the goddess in me couldn't. I found ways to fly during turbulence, while going against the wind. He began to tell himself stories he believed were true, in order to avoid being held accountable for his own actions and behaviors that caused the consequences he was now dealing with. He believed his own lies in order to feel better about himself while continuing to blame me for his problems. Does this sound familiar to you? It's not your fault; don't believe their lies. Instead, believe the truth about you and begin to love you more. That powerful self-love will transcend above anything and anyone that is trying to keep you from becoming the best you and getting the life you deserve and want. Life is too short to spend it unhappy and unsure.

22

Life Interrupted:
SOMETHING'S GOT A HOLD ON ME

I VOWED TO NEVER look back when I said goodbye to my marriage. I said I'd never settle again. This was my second chance at love and this time I was playing for keeps. I would take note of all the lessons learned and not repeat them again. Instead, I would use them to my advantage. They were my greatest lessons and in spite of all of the pain, they were my greatest blessings. All of a sudden, my past relationships and ex-lovers, who I hadn't seen in a decade or two, came across my life. "How ironic," I thought. "Could this just be a coincidence?" It appeared innocent enough, so I played with the idea of possibly rekindling an old flame or two, but then I started noticing patterns in each of them. Most had absolutely nothing to offer and some were in transition periods and had gone back to live with their mom and dad. Their priorities were having the nicest cars and freshest clothes, while trying to impress others by overcompensating for the unsatisfied lives they were living. Or were they satisfied? Were they truly comfortable living this way? Still selling drugs in their mid-thirties and complaining about child support? As much as I toyed with illusions of falling in love with childhood romances and living happily ever after, something wasn't right. There were red flags such as, quick fuses, conversations that led nowhere, and futures that weren't planned. I thought about my own life and how I had worked hard and sacrificed for the things I had earned. Why was I attracting this type of man? Did old habits really die hard even after I said I didn't want them anymore? I didn't feel like I was what I attracted because I was living my life opposite of theirs. Yet, there was something very familiar that we all had in common: Not knowing our value.

Even after I gained the strength and courage to leave a toxic relationship, some of the damage remained and it was apparent I was still comfortable with the familiar instead of doing the real work to love and value myself more than anyone else could. I needed to reinvent myself in order to rid myself of old habits and thoughts that held me hostage for years. And just like that I let go of the need for male companionship like cold turkey. Don't get me wrong, I am not saying I don't need a man. What I am saying is that I don't need a man to fill any void God himself can't fill. I didn't need a man to validate who I was or make me feel complete. I needed to love and commit to myself the very things I wanted in order for me to receive that kind of love and commitment back. I had to let go of every behavior and illusion that didn't line up with what I truly wanted no matter if it felt lonely. I had to truly trust God and have faith that he would send my Mr. Right when the time was right. In that moment the time wasn't right; the time was convenient, but I needed more than convenience, I needed the real deal. Waiting for Mr. Right allowed me to drop everything in me and around me that needed to be left. Something had a hold on me and I chose to get free.

23

Life Interrupted:
DEATH

MY MOTHER AND I were on our annual vacation as mother and daughter. We chose a cruise this time, rather than traveling to one destination by plane. We were sailing and island hopping on the beautiful islands of Cozumel, Mahogany Bay, Isla Roatan and Belize for eight days. It felt like paradise on the Carnival Dream ship that was packed with celebrity entertainment and daily concerts. It felt good to get away from it all, until the day we ported back to New Orleans. Since we had been in "international waters" we hadn't received any incoming calls, texts, or voicemails. The internet package we bought had been unstable with very limited use. We were eating breakfast on the ship when I received a direct message on my Instagram account from one of my brother's friends. She asked me to call her regarding an emergency with my brother. At the time I couldn't call, and there was nothing I could do about it. As we travelled closer to land, my text messages started coming through and I received one from my estranged husband that I will never be able to forget. It said, "Your brother died last night."

I screamed, "Oh, my God," and jumped up from the table where my mother and her friends were dining. I frantically made my way back to our cabin with tears in my eyes calling on Jesus' name. My mother's friends followed me, attempting to hold up my mother, who was extremely weak upon hearing the news of her son. I called my estranged husband and asked him what happened. "What the fuck are you talking about?" I was in disbelief. The tears and cries of agony overcame the room and I handed my mom the cell phone because I was overwhelmed with grief. She continued to listen to him as he explained the situation and in that moment our dream vacation turned into a nightmare. My only sibling and her only son had passed away the day before and we hadn't known, nor could we have been there with him. I immediately felt guilty. This was the one time when I couldn't save him.

We took an emergency flight from New Orleans to Atlanta to claim the body and get it transported back to our hometown in Florida for a proper service. Our lives were interrupted in a way that I had never felt before. It was a pain so deep, it's indescribable. I cried myself to sleep for days, and every time I closed my eyes, I saw visions and memories of him. I swam in my tears and tried to comprehend how and why my brother's life had ended. He was someone who continually fell, but always managed to get back up again and make his way to the light. Only God knew the why behind the what, so I stopped questioning his death. I tried my best to release the pain and feel his presence, so it wouldn't feel like he was truly gone. His comedic attitude was what I truly longed for and I wondered who was going to make me laugh when things became too serious. Who was going to relish in my "blonde moments"? Who were my daughter's going to call Uncle? The little big brother that I always tried to protect, I just wanted to resurrect. I felt alone, really alone, and I was left here to take care of our broken-hearted mother whose strength was generally that of an ox, but this seemed like too much for her to endure. There was a hole in my stomach, like a part of me was missing and it was. It felt like a part of my heart was gone forever and I felt like an angel with a broken wing. Death is never easy, but it is something we all will have to face at some point in our lives.

As unexpected as my brother's death was, I was able to finally find some peace. I had to thank God for the thirty-four years he allowed him to be on this Earth and realized that God needed him more. Although I had watched over him most of our lives, it was now his time to watch over us. I felt my brother's presence even through the pain and became inspired even more to finish what I'd started. I pursued my dreams relentlessly and didn't let anything hinder me. I heard my brother tell me to fly, even if I was only flying with one wing.

I asked God to please let me find my brother's spirit in the most beautiful places. The sounds of the ocean or where still waters run deep. Let me find him in the flowers blossoming in the spring, or as the leaves change colors in the fall. Let me see him through my daughters' bright eyes, as they ask questions and I search for answers to provide them with.

My daughters didn't understand what was happening. This was their first experience losing someone close to them that they loved and adored, and once they saw his lifeless body in the casket, their pain was indescribable. They had so many questions, which I didn't have the answers to and I asked God for strength to help get my family through. Day by day I began to realize his life and labor of love was not in vain, and it was up to me to carry on his legacy through my life's work. My life shifted immediately in that moment, and I vowed to not spend another second of my life anywhere unhappy, around negative people, or distracted from my purpose. This thing was working out for my good, and as soon as I grasped that concept I started to rise from the ashes. I wanted to live on purpose with every ounce to give. May his legacy be left to those of us who still live.

Don't let death grip you in pain, despair, or fear. Instead, allow it to propel you into your purpose and continue to carry on as your loved one would have liked you to. A loved one's death can be used as fuel for your fire when you realize life is but a vapor. Here today and gone tomorrow, we should live everyday like it's our last. Don't settle for less and don't tolerate any situation, circumstance, or person that doesn't see how valuable you are. Life is too short to be anything but happy.

24

Life Interrupted:
I REMEMBER

I REMEMBER IN KINDERGARTEN I had to lead the class speech and I heard you yell out my name from the audience because you were so proud of me. You

were at the tender age of two or three, and as the audience burst out in laughter, I searched for you in the stands. I couldn't find you, but from that moment on I knew you were my best friend. You always cheered me on and watched me live my life with admiration. Most of the time I wasn't living for me, I was living for you. I wanted to really make it and had visions of major success, so I could come back and get you. To see you at the top is all I wanted, but of course I imagined you'd always be with me. I wanted you to have the best, but God decided you needed rest.

My brother loved his mother and father. We shared fond memories of being in the kitchen, the heartbeat of the home, while our mother baked cakes. One day she asked us a question. I believe he was five and I was eight at the time. The question was, "What ingredient is this cake missing?" She gave us samples and my brother yelled out, "Moisture!" He was the funniest character you'd ever meet, for he had the gift of laughter. There wasn't a time in my life that I didn't try to protect him; no matter if it was sibling rivalry to toughen him up, or me driving a hundred miles an hour to come to his rescue. Our relationship was and still is a special bond. Your death was not in vain. It's one we're taking in strides.

He gave me the motivation and strength I needed to finish what I started. His smile and jokes would light up a room and every soul he came across felt connected to him. He lived a life as free as he could be, teaching me to not take life so seriously. I thank him for never judging me, or anyone else he knew. His free spirit was why everyone who surrounded him loved him. We could be ourselves without reservation, and we knew we had a friend, family member, and brother we could run to without hesitation.

God needed you more than we did, so I won't be selfish because I know this isn't the end. It's only an ending to your Earth's chapter, but when I get to where you are I bet we will greet each other with laughter. I'm sure he's in heaven, clowning around, singing like Beyoncé, and telling the angels they have crooked halos. God himself, with a big sense of humor, sees his reflection in you with so much pride, and I rest in the fact that you'll always be by his side. There's no more pain or drama where you are now, just peace and love that this world needs. Give it to us in moments as we reminisce. Give it to us in happiness and bliss. Give it to us when we miss you most. Give it to us when we start to boast. I know you'll give it to us when we're down. We all have memories of how you were such a clown.

I'm now flying with one broken wing, but don't worry; I'm going to fly regardless and so will everyone else. Your spirit will never die my dear brother because each of us has parts of you that connects us to each other. Buddha once said, "Thousands of candles can be lighted from a single candle, and the life of the candle will not be shortened. Happiness never decreases by being shared." We will share and spread your happiness and love. Live on through us Jason Paul White, we love you.

Dear Reader,

THANK YOU FOR reading this book. It shows that you are ready for change and willing to allow a shift to take place in your life because normal isn't working anymore. As human beings we are called to transform the world and not conform to it. This means taking a stand for your core values and beliefs, so much that you're willing to let go of every toxic person, place, or thing in order to get there. When you take a stand, you stand out. You view the world through a different set of lenses and have the ability to light up dark places. This will come with much resistance, especially from those closest to you. They love the old you, the same you, the you that stayed stagnant like them. You were like a mirror to them and as long as they could see their reflection in you that was good enough for them. I've come to let you know that you don't have to live for anyone other than yourself and the people you were called to serve. In order for that to happen God has a purpose for you that only you are equipped to complete. This means letting go of every agenda someone else had for you or even the life you planned.

We all go through things that awaken us to this transformative process. For some it's a divorce and the life you knew has taken such a turn that you're not sure if you can survive on your own. A failed relationship is one of life's greatest lessons. It teaches us to use caution in our future relationships and it shows us the parts we played in the demise of it. When we're really mature we evolve from it and become better versions of ourselves: preparing our hearts, minds, and souls for the next relationship if we want it. However, you could choose to be single, not because you're scared of another failed relationship, but because you learned you're better off dating and not committing to anyone other than yourself. There's nothing wrong with that. Singlehood comes with a freedom that allows you to love yourself and others without rules or restrictions. The interruption from a divorce comes so you'll know how to love yourself without feeling like you needed someone to love you first. It also reminds you that you can do what you thought you couldn't do alone. I'm not advocating divorce, but I am advocating self-love before attempting to love others more than yourself. If you're not willing to love yourself first, you will become devastated if your significant other leaves.

Maybe some of you have lost a friend or family member and you're so stricken with grief that you become depressed, thinking you'll never see the light of day. The death of a loved one teaches us to really value the beauty of life each day. If you choose to change your perspective from loss to gain the universe will respond, and as you reach a better quality of life and insightful purpose, a heart of gratitude comes with being alive each day. You begin to live with purpose, with the intent to leave a legacy for generations. After all, we don't last forever, but your life's work can.

Life Interrupted could also mean transitioning from one job to another, which sometimes makes you feel inferior because you're starting over in a new place. You're surrounded by a different culture and people you don't know, but that's the exciting part because you're challenged to stretch yourself outside of your comfort zone and learn something new. Healthy working relationships can be fostered by adding value to your new team and receiving the value they add in return. This was one of the things I lacked in my previous job, which was a fear based environment. There was no opportunity for advancement because everyone was out for themselves and competed with one another. Insecurities were at an all-time high and morale at an astonishing low. The best thing I ever did for myself was resign and accept a position in management. Although I'd never been in a similar position before, I embraced it because I knew God called me to it. There are many days you'll feel like you don't know what you're doing, but as long as you're willing to learn and expand your horizons you will overcome any obstacle and experience a new-found confidence.

Life Interrupted for addicts means learning not to depend on a substance that makes you high and numbs the cares of this world. Instead, it's for you to open your eyes, serve the world, and realize you are powerful beyond measure. You harness enough power to be happy and at peace with whatever comes your way because at any given moment life can change, and you must be strong enough to adapt to the changes. Life is often interrupted with changes not to hurt you, but to help you. Your soul surrenders to new possibilities while training your mind to let go of what was, in order to embrace what is. We cannot hold onto our past, nor can we become victims of it. Furthermore, we cannot depend on how things use to be, in order to shape how things could be. When transitioning from one level to the next, it's life's way of interrupting our comfort zones by bringing us to an unfamiliar place. When you're in that place you'll be challenged to grow, think differently, and change your behavior. Each new level requires humbleness, perseverance, faith, and a sense of gratitude because you're accomplishing things you never have before, which lifts you higher. When you make up in your mind to rid yourself of people who aren't going anywhere, and serve no purpose in your life, there's a release of dead weight as you gain freedom to live life the way you want to. Your ability to believe in yourself opens up the possibilities of new relationships and divine opportunities. I am extremely blessed to have friends and acquaintances in my life that support, love, and challenge me to be the best me. Don't settle for people that only want you to be the person they desire you to be. Life is too short to be ordinary. Allow it to be interrupted and become extraordinary. After all, you are.

THE AUTHOR

Keri Steward was born and raised in Jacksonville, Florida, where she found a love for reading, speaking, and sports. She used the gift of gab and her athletic abilities throughout her high school years and graduated from Jean Ribault Sr. High School in 1997. That fall, she moved to Tallahassee to attend Florida State University, where she became Assistant Editor for The Florida State Times newspaper while pursuing her college education. One day on campus, she met a young lady who unlocked more potential inside of her that she hadn't realized she had. At the young woman's request, Keri tried out for an on-campus modeling troupe that would later birth her modeling career. Keri graduated from Florida State University in 2002 and continued her modeling career throughout young adulthood to grace runways, international hair shows, magazines, book covers, calendars, and commercials as a way to express her artistic side. In 2014 she received her Master's Degree with a concentration in Human Resources Management from the University of Phoenix. Keri currently resides in Atlanta, Georgia, where she works as an author, part time model, and full time Human Resources Manager. Her greatest achievements are her two daughters Nalani Steward, whose name means "The Heavens," and Kennedi Steward whose name means "Little sister." Giving life to them was the beginning of Keri's life being interrupted for the better.

Keri continues to involve herself in non-profit organizations such as OneSight, which allowed her to travel the world in order to help others see. This is Keri's mission in life: to not only help others see physically, but spiritually and mentally as well. Vision is a basic human right and by providing access to those who lack the resources, a transformative process begins that immediately enhances the quality of life. Keri also works with American Kidney Services (AKS), a local, non-profit, Atlanta charity that strives to help kidney disease sufferers, who are in financial need. Hope House for Domestic violence is a charity Keri is also passionate about because it is a program outreach focusing on single women and mothers with children transitioning from domestic violence situations. Hope House (HOPE4DV) is partnering with local domestic violence shelters to assist with "next steps," including residence, employment, childcare, education, goal-setting, and much more. The goal is to provide tools for empowerment: mind, body, and spirit.

Keri believes, as a part of the human race, we all have the responsibility to help someone else in need. Oftentimes, others see things we can't see in ourselves. It is Keri's belief that we come across divine connections in our lives on the way to our destinies, in order to become the person we were intended to be. Always look for divine connections and opportunities.

Notes

CPSIA information can be obtained
at www.ICGtesting.com
Printed in the USA
BVHW092127220819
556538BV00004B/81/P